Motherhood is about the sculpting ... McNiel hands you desperately neede... formation of your family—but for y... a holy, needful work through the pages you noid in your hands.

ANN VOSKAMP
Mother of seven and author of *New York Times* bestsellers *The Broken Way* and *One Thousand Gifts*

Catherine has written so beautifully of a woman's spiritual pathway to God. She has found the words to express what so many of us experience: repetitiveness of service that becomes a mysterious celebration of the sacredness of life and the presence of God. I wish I had written this book myself: a book that celebrates the spaghetti days of family, the wonder of pregnancy and birthing, and, above all, the sacredness of the journey.

VALERIE BELL
President and CEO of AWANA and author of *Getting Out of Your Kids' Faces and Into Their Hearts* and *Faith-Shaped Kids*

Writing in the tradition of Brother Lawrence, Catherine McNiel shows readers how to keep company with God in the everyday. But she is no monastic. She is a mother, caught in the turbulence of life with small children. How I wish I'd had this book—and her example—when I was just beginning my journey into motherhood.

JEN POLLOCK MICHEL
Author of the award-winning book *Teach Us to Want*

Here's a book for every Christian parent forced to smile through an exhortation to "enjoy every moment; it's all over so fast!" Catherine McNiel doesn't urge you to "make time for God" in early parenting but rather to see God there already: in the trial, in the joy, in the leaky diapers, plugged ducts, and scraped knees. Instead of being one more call to "sleep when the baby sleeps," her book can help a weary parent wake up a bit more to the eternal life they're living.

TED OLSEN
Director of editorial development, *Christianity Today*

Catherine's words are nothing short of a banquet table of nourishment for a hungry mama's soul. *Long Days of Small Things* invites the reader to see the mundane tasks of motherhood (changing diapers, folding laundry, planning meals, etc.) not as interruptions to our spiritual life, but as an oft-overlooked path closer to Jesus. Accept Catherine's invitation, mom. Read and be seen, feel valued, and awaken to the beautiful, spiritual practice of motherhood.

AUBREY SAMPSON
Author of Overcomer: *Breaking Down the Walls of Shame and Rebuilding Your Soul*

Moms, if you don't have time to read a book, this is the book for you! If you hunger to connect to God, these words will nourish your deep places. On every page you will be reminded that your children don't distract you from the way—they are the way to a richer, more meaningful life. Offering simple doable practices to connect to God, McNiel's beautifully woven words will strengthen you for your journey.

MARGOT STARBUCK
Author of *Small Things with Great Love: Adventures in Loving Your Neighbor*

Long Days of Small Things is a mom's welcomed guide to finding grace in each moment. Writing profoundly about the wonder of creating and nurturing a new human life, Catherine McNiel explains simple ways to practice God's presence in daily routines. These practical suggestions put worship within reach of every busy mom, gently explaining how to live in the present to find God in the chaos of chasing kids. This book will change how you view motherhood. It will change how you view life!

JAN AND MARK FOREMAN
Authors of *Never Say No: Raising Big-Picture Kids*

When my six children were small, I often thought I needed peace and space to grow my spirit. Wrong. God had six teachers in front of me all along. What I really needed was McNiel's book to open my eyes to the miraculous presence of God already in front of me. What a spectacular guide into the holy daily labor of loving our kids.

LESLIE LEYLAND FIELDS
Author of *Crossing the Waters: Following Jesus through the Storms, the Fish, the Doubt, and the Seas*

For many long centuries the disciplined spiritual life has been largely defined by religious communities and leaders who are predominantly male. Cut off from the presence of young families—crying infants, riotous children, nursing mothers—the spiritual disciplines we've been taught are generally about cultivating the life of the mind. What happens when a mom like Catherine McNiel enters the conversation? A delightful introduction into a whole new world of incarnational disciplines that take the body seriously. We are bodies; we take care of others' bodies. And in the daily stuff of embodiment, Catherine reminds us, is where we can meet our incarnational God.

SARAH ARTHUR
Coauthor of *The Year of Small Things: Radical Faith for the Rest of Us*

Long Days of Small Things is a gift to all of us householders. Catherine's patient and generous wisdom shines a light into the sleepless nights of parenting to reveal the spiritual work happening when we're busy cleaning up soggy Cheerios and endless glasses of spilled milk. I want to give this to every mom I know, to say, "Good job, brave mom. You're in the trenches of what matters most."

TRICIA LOTT WILLIFORD
Author of *Let's Pretend We're Normal, And Life Comes Back,* and *You Can Do This*

When I was a mother of three young children, there was never enough time for spiritual disciplines like Bible study, prayer, worship, and service. I came to realize I was chasing a shimmering false image of spiritual growth instead of living fully in the company of my heavenly Father. Catherine McNiel offers mothers a freeing, wise invitation to grow deep roots in the rich soil of family life. She connects some of the classic spiritual disciplines to the embodied realities of parenting. Her wise, thoughtful words and eminently practical suggestions will help you flourish in the presence of God during those long days with little ones. Highly recommended.

MICHELLE VAN LOON
Author of *Moments & Days: How Our Holy Celebrations Shape Our Faith*

Catherine's well-crafted prose will leave you wanting more, while the weight behind her words—words that underscore all you already have and are—will entice you to reread entire paragraphs five times. *Long Days of Small Things* is a timeless gem, celebrating the beauty of motherhood in fresh, profound ways.

JESSIE MINASSIAN
Author, speaker, and mother

Catherine McNiel claims that motherhood is a spiritual discipline. In this beautiful book, she demonstrates that parenting is holy and transformative—from the incarnational glory of childbearing to the trying tedium of sleepless nights. McNiel writes with the grace and confidence of a midwife, and *Long Days of Small Things* is just that—a work of spiritual midwifery that will comfort, encourage, and strengthen mothers.

KATHERINE WILLIS PERSHEY
Author of *Very Married: Field Notes on Love and Fidelity*

Long Days of Small Things

CATHERINE McNIEL

Long Days of Small Things

MOTHERHOOD AS
A SPIRITUAL DISCIPLINE

A NavPress resource published in alliance
with Tyndale House Publishers, Inc.

NavPress is the publishing ministry of The Navigators, an international Christian organization and leader in personal spiritual development. NavPress is committed to helping people grow spiritually and enjoy lives of meaning and hope through personal and group resources that are biblically rooted, culturally relevant, and highly practical.

For more information, visit www.NavPress.com.

Long Days of Small Things: Motherhood as a Spiritual Discipline

Copyright © 2017 by Catherine McNiel. All rights reserved.

A NavPress resource published in alliance with Tyndale House Publishers, Inc.

NAVPRESS and the NAVPRESS logo are registered trademarks of NavPress, The Navigators, Colorado Springs, CO. *TYNDALE* is a registered trademark of Tyndale House Publishers, Inc. Absence of ® in connection with marks of NavPress or other parties does not indicate an absence of registration of those marks.

The Team:
Don Pape, Publisher
Caitlyn Carlson, Acquisitions and Developmental Editor
Nicole Grimes, Designer

Cover photograph taken by Julie Chen. Copyright © Tyndale House Publishers, Inc. All rights reserved.
Cover photograph of paper texture copyright © zephyr_p/Adobe Stock. All rights reserved.
Cover Ilustration of flourish by Michael Cina/Adobe Creative Cloud. All rights reserved.
Interior illustration of grunge texture copyright © snb2087/Adobe Stock. All rights reserved.

Published in association with the literary agent Don Gates of The Gates Group, www.the-gates -group.com.

Some of the anecdotal illustrations in this book are true to life and are included with the permission of the persons involved. All other illustrations are composites of real situations, and any resemblance to people living or dead is purely coincidental.

For information about special discounts for bulk purchases, please contact Tyndale House Publishers at csresponse@tyndale.com or call 800-323-9400.

Cataloging-in-Publication Data is available.

ISBN 978-1-63146-643-4

Printed in the United States of America

23   22   21   20   19   18   17
7   6   5   4   3   2   1

For my beautiful, life-giving mother, Linda.
Without you, and all you are,
none of this could have happened.

And for Asher, Benjamin, and Selah.
You completely stole my muse,
and I am the better for it.

Contents

BEFORE WE BEGIN XV

CHAPTER 1
REDEMPTION: FINDING THE HOUSEHOLDERS' PATH 1
Redemption in Practice: Breathe | Walk | Be

CHAPTER 2
CONSECRATION: SHE CARRIED GOD UNDER HER HEART 17
Consecration in Practice:
Eating and Drinking | Cooking | Household Tasks

CHAPTER 3
CREATION: WITH THE HELP OF GOD I CREATED A MAN! 35
Creation in Practice: Menstruation | Sex | Awakening

CHAPTER 4
INCARNATION: FLOWING WITH MILK AND HONEY 55
Incarnation in Practice: Body | Breastfeeding | Water

CHAPTER 5
NURTURE: MADE IN THE IMAGE OF GOD'S LOVE 75
Nurture in Practice: Cherish | Discipline | Sleep

CHAPTER 6
SERVICE & SOLITUDE: ALL-NIGHTERS WITH GOD 97
Service and Solitude in Practice: Silence | Diapers | Work

CHAPTER 7

SACRIFICE & SURRENDER: FEASTING WITH OPEN HANDS 115

Sacrifice and Surrender in Practice: Pain | Driving | Clutter

CHAPTER 8

PERSEVERANCE: SWEET GRAPES 135

Perseverance in Practice: Routine | Gratitude | Music

CHAPTER 9

CELEBRATION: ALIVE AND AWAKE 157

Celebration in Practice: See | Hear | Touch

ONE LAST THING . . . 177

ACKNOWLEDGMENTS 179

NOTES 183

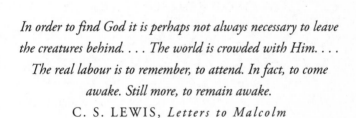

In order to find God it is perhaps not always necessary to leave the creatures behind. . . . The world is crowded with Him. . . . The real labour is to remember, to attend. In fact, to come awake. Still more, to remain awake.

C. S. LEWIS, *Letters to Malcolm*

Before We Begin

CAN I MAKE A CONFESSION?

I am not *that mom* on Facebook who has it all together, peacefully raising perfect children. You'll never find me Instagramming my latest parenting triumph or pinning pretzel-and-kiwi Easter bunnies to Pinterest.

I don't even have a Pinterest account.

I'm the mom yelling across the yard loudly enough to wake the whole neighborhood. The one who doesn't manage to grab a shower and would never consider rising before her crack-of-dawn children.

I serve birthday cake out of a 9x13 pan, and my kids go to church in striped pants and paisley shirts (dirty ones, too, with mismatched socks). My runaway bag is packed, and I'm always just one more tantrum away from using it. I never manage to find the peace in the chaos. I long for serenity and fall to pieces in the mayhem.

I am not winning at motherhood.

But—and I take a long, slow breath with this life-changing

but—I believe, with all my heart, that every department-store meltdown is cultivating my soul into something strong and beautiful. I cling to a deep and certain conviction that motherhood is *in and of itself* a spiritual practice—that the Creator of wombs and breasts placed deep spiritual fruit into the seasons and tasks of motherhood. That we're not meant to add more "shoulds" to our schedule, more work to allow us into God's presence. That instead our Father beckons us to simply awaken and see the spiritual disciplines *we already perform each day.*

Love, joy, peace, patience, kindness, goodness, faithfulness, gentleness, and self-control—we may not realize it, but a harvest is being formed in our souls as we ebb and flow through sleepless nights and chaotic days. Just as certainly and invisibly as the seeds in my garden somehow turn into carrots and potatoes out of sight, below the surface our spirits are being formed in the secret corners of motherhood.

Don't think that I find it easy. The pieces don't fall right into place for me. Nobody could mistake me for a modern-day Madonna, presiding over my cherubic angels. No, this journey strikes me as spiritual because I am so flawed it simply *must* be. If this trial by fire does not burn away my edges, nothing will.

Here is my invitation: Walk with me in these pages through daily life, with all its beauty and pain. We'll look honestly at the journey of motherhood and the spiritual fruit that hides there. To keep it real, following each chapter are three "practices" we're already doing—things like breathing, washing dishes, and driving the car—with practical tips on how these everyday tasks can shape our spirits.

You'll recognize all the landmarks, the highs and the lows, but it can be difficult to notice how powerful and life-giving they are when we're in the thick of it all. We're walking together this time, so we can help each other see along the way.[1]

So let's journey together as we labor and deliver our children, day after day after day. Whether we birthed or adopted our children, the labor and delivery never really stops, does it? We mamas pour ourselves out from beginning to end so that others may have life. This pouring-out is a rich spiritual practice, if we awaken to it. And since we are *doing* it already, all that remains for us is to breathe deeply and begin to drink.

My prayer is that in these pages you will glimpse, occasionally, this beautiful something always lurking in the chaos and the struggle.

I'm convinced it is God himself, waiting right here where he made you.

Will you join me?

---

[1] Since I'm speaking to *you*, sister, I'll use words like *mothers*. But it's important you understand that I'm not excluding men or implying that our responsibilities are "women's work." I hope men are reading along! Many dads walk a nearly identical parenting journey right beside us and are being shaped spiritually by the everyday, just as we are. So to every dad reading this book, welcome. We're so grateful to be in the thick of this with you.

CHAPTER I

REDEMPTION

Finding the Householders' Path

I WEAVE MY WAY through the crowded sanctuary, crying baby in the sling. I'm earnestly trying to get out of the church service and into the "cry" room before the fussing becomes screaming. His little eyes are closed, but his crumpled face is beet red. With cheeks rubbing frantically against my chest, he's winding up for a major demonstration. I walk faster.

When you have small children, going anywhere can seem like more trouble than it's worth. Church is no exception: a lot of hassle in order to perform the same childcare tasks in a less conducive environment. We are visitors at this church today. I long to be present, focused, and engaged. Instead, this outing becomes one more opportunity to be banished from adult teaching and corporate worship.

Finding the right room, I pause and read the sign on the door: *Breastfeeding Mothers Only*. My heart sinks. Not only am I to be relegated to a closet with a demanding baby, but my sex and lactation determine that I am the only one in the family who can be. No chance of Daddy or Grandma taking a shift later, I guess. I put a resentful hand on the knob and push the door open.

My senses and emotions flood before my mind has a chance to take it in. The setting offers itself immediately as sanctuary. The room is dimly lit, perfect for soothing a child—or a mama's soul. The furniture is nice, comfortable. All my needs are anticipated: nursing pillows and tissue, a water pitcher and glasses. A silver tray is laid out for Communion, awaiting my participation. Next to it is a plaque that reads, "*Mother, what you have given in love has become part of me. I thank God always for you.*"

Immediately tears are rolling down my face. I hadn't known that I felt invisible until I felt seen. I hadn't realized how thankless the ceaseless sacrifices of motherhood felt until someone gently pointed me to their honor and value.

Missed Adventures

I've always been a bookworm, and quite of few of my childhood BFFs were fictional. Frodo and Sam. Arthur and Merlin. My imagination was ignited as I lived through their adventures, but when I tried to picture *myself* in their stories, I just couldn't. The hero and his buddies were usually male; the womenfolk stayed back at camp during the real adventure. In all likelihood these women were having their own meaningful experiences, but *those* stories didn't make the book. It dawned on me that in my favorite epics, had I been there, I wouldn't *be* there. Without knowing it, I had imbibed a love of courage and inspiration—and a suspicion that there are beautiful places and quests to which women are not invited.

My life outside the pages, however, has seen no end of adventures. Topping the list is this miracle I've been caught up in for the past ten years: creating, birthing, and nurturing three brand-new souls. My children.

But as almost any mom can tell you, it's easy to get lost along the way. We're often playing the role of those who stayed behind to tend the fire, those whose stories fade into history untold and unsung. Again and again we stumble upon the message that the demands of motherhood will keep us from the most thrilling excursions.

Spiritual journeys, for instance. Investing time and energy into seeking God and his presence throughout the day. Loving and serving others in his name. Fellowshipping joyfully in community.

This is one adventure that does not drop easily from my hands. It haunts me like a song I can't place, like a delicious scent wafting on the winds of memory. It is the ambition I cannot quite let die.

Do you feel this too? Do you ache to connect with God, to love and serve others well? Does your soul long to be filled—and yet finds itself drying up in the busy stretches of every long day? When motherhood leaves us parched, where are we to find the time and energy for such a quest?

True and lasting spiritual growth comes from practicing spiritual disciplines over time, as Christian teaching and generations of seekers can attest. Our goal isn't to earn God's love or catch his attention, but to exercise and build our spiritual muscles. By investing our time and energy in pursuing God, our hearts and minds are changed; we begin to find him, to make a place for him in our spirits, our thoughts, and our identity.

Richard Foster's important book *Celebration of Discipline* outlines twelve practices that form the backbone of such a life: meditation, prayer, fasting, study, simplicity, solitude, submission, service, confession, worship, guidance, and celebration.[1] Before becoming a mother, I eagerly embraced as many of these as my responsibilities allowed.

Now, my responsibilities rarely allow me to take a shower, much less sharpen spiritual practices. Silence and solitude? Never, ever, day or night. Prayer? Harder than you'd think after years of sleep deprivation. Fasting? Not while pregnant or breastfeeding. Service? Well, my kids definitely left their mark that time we "helped" at community painting day. Worship? There were years I didn't attend a worship service without a toddler bouncing on my back.

As mothers, our accumulated experience speaks a compelling case: Pursuing a deep spiritual life is simply not possible in this season, at least not in the ways we were taught. It seems the spiritual quest is one place where mothers, at least, cannot go.

That, or I'm really botching it.

Doorways and Forgotten Paths

I'm ready to leave the shop, but one thing stands in my way—the door. Not exactly a formidable barrier, but the odds are against me. My preschooler is running in circles, while my toddler pulls at my left hand. My right hand grips this terribly unwieldy baby carrier. Inside the carrier is, of course, my infant daughter. She is hungry and tired and howling. My purse is falling off one shoulder, my diaper bag off the other. Children are asking about snacks and water fountains, and I'm wondering, *How are we all going to get through that door?*

No one jumps to hold it open for me, though more than enough people are watching to ensure my embarrassment when I attempt to hold it for myself. Myself, that is, and my entourage: these three precious ones who know life only through my own life, who see me as the primary source of all things. Somehow, with bags crashing down against my forearms, I bang open the door with my hip, weave the toddler under one arm, and lift the baby carrier over the preschooler's head. Somehow, we all stumble through before it closes on any small fingers or toes.

Yes, ladies and gentlemen, I have done it. I have walked through a door.

Later that day I read an article about a Christian teacher I deeply admire. The writer described this hero-of-the-faith as so spiritually enlightened, he radiated peace just by walking through the door.

This stops me in my tracks. It testifies mightily against me, against the fruit of my life in this season. I'm not *quite* the picture of enlightenment. If radiating peace (with or without a door) is the measure of spiritual success, I'm certain I'll never arrive.

———•••———

A few months before my door-opening heroics, I stole away into adult world for a weekend to attend a Christian conference. In the hot, crowded room, the speaker drove his point home with passion: If we have a genuine commitment to knowing God, we must spend at least an hour each day in silence and solitude.

There I was, ground to a halt once again. About to birth my third child in five years (the soon-to-be daughter in the infant carrier), I hadn't slept through the night or gone to the bathroom by myself anytime in recent memory. My physical body housed a tiny tenant; I was literally inseparable from this beloved person I nurtured. This simple suggestion of solitude—one I would have recommended myself in a different season—stole my breath away.

I didn't hear anything else at the conference, because these words reverberated through my ears and soul for weeks, drowning out everything else. The list of spiritual disciplines no longer feasible to me as a mother grows longer with each new child. And, of course, any thought of silence and solitude is a happy dream mostly forgotten.

No one tries to exclude mothers from the "spiritual life," but it happens regardless. I hear laments rising up in the hearts of mothers, mourning the losses that this season of nurturing unexpectedly brings: the impossibility of pursuing something soul-creative, something life-giving. *There's no time, space, energy, or money. We'll have to wait until the children are older. Right now I just can't.*

And yet. Underneath my unwashed hair and sleepy eyes, the truth is undeniable: These days have been made out of miracles. Uniquely and utterly *female* miracles. Pregnancy, labor, delivery, newborn days, and nurturing growing children have taken me to places where *only* women and mothers can go. These fundamental experiences are inescapably feminine, not experienced by all women but by *only women.* If our daily experiences are so entirely singular, why shouldn't our spiritual disciplines be uniquely suited to us as well?

So now, almost a decade into the most grueling journey of selfless giving and sacrifice I can imagine, my spirit is fighting back. *There must be another path.*

Children are consuming. They leave us with nothing left to give ourselves or anyone else. But this is the perfect training ground for our spirits, the very setting many disciplines are designed to produce. Our demanding, beloved children *are* what we create—they *are* our spiritual path. What if we looked through new eyes and discovered that into our very life stages our Creator has placed impressions of himself, reflections of his strength and beauty, a spiritual path laid out just for us?

———•·——

People who walk serenely through doorways are rarely surrounded by children. In fact, those who achieve acclaim for their great accomplishments of faith rarely spend their days birthing, nursing, and raising families.

Jesus loved children, spent time with them, and instructed his followers to be like them. But he wasn't raising them. Moses, the apostle Paul, C. S. Lewis, Mother Teresa, Saint Francis, Martin Luther, Thomas Merton—none of these people spent their days raising children.

And yet, what else is so enlightening, so character-sharpening, so weakness-illuminating, and so virtue-defining as the nonstop practice of self-sacrifice and surrender that defines motherhood? If a deep, rich spiritual life requires personal time and space, most people throughout history—hard workers living in crowded homes, striving to care for their families and just barely getting by—are simply out of luck.

Immersed now in these long days of small things, I understand why so few women traveled with Sam and Frodo, Arthur and Merlin: They were very, very busy. For most of human history, women began bearing children as young teenagers, then went on to be pregnant or nursing for the bulk of their lives. Imagine the wisdom, the understanding, and the spiritual depth that was fashioned in the souls of these women as they emptied themselves day in and day out, body and soul, often giving up their lives in the making and birthing of babies. These women were constantly in the grips of life and death, searching and expanding the depths of human love and spirit, chasing toddlers, trying to gather enough food to sustain a family, feeling babies kick their bladders and ribs, mourning loss after incomparable loss, nurturing life after precious life.

Their years revolved around surrender, sacrifice, service, and perseverance. They acted out the signature works of God in their bodies: creation, new life, and redemption. Though the spiritual adventures of these mothers—close to the campfire and far from the fires of Mordor—did not make the pages of epic tales, their seasons and practices tell a deeply spiritual story.

But each day has enough trouble of its own, doesn't it? When we're in the thick of things, it's hard to see the bigger picture.

Some religions, such as Hinduism and Buddhism, have a name for people in this predicament: *householders*. Recognizing that folks can't just up and leave their spouses or children, these religions give householders a different set of expectations. Rather than becoming meditating monks, studying under gurus and wandering alone through the forest, householders are asked, for now, simply to be faithful in responsibility.

Though we mamas may appear half crazed, sleep-deprived, harried, and unkempt, our souls are being taught and sharpened and purified. I'm sure of it. We're not able to sit and ponder this, or even be aware of it most of the time. But soul refining is the work of struggle, sacrifice, discomfort, and perseverance. My three whirling dervishes take me to the end of myself on a daily basis, and I'm certain my soul will emerge stronger for it.

Maybe Mommy Boot Camp cultivates a soul even better than spending these years in constant meditation.

———•••———

The morning I ran out of the church sanctuary with a loud, hungry infant, my heart sank when I read the words *Breastfeeding Mothers Only*. My experiences and disappointments taught me that the services required by motherhood meant my spirit must go without. Instead, that day I opened the door to something far different from anything I had ever heard preached or described before, something available only to mothers. Not a "make do" or "Plan B" sort of path, but something unique and honored, inherently spiritual and inherently "mother." Far from being relegated to a closet, I nursed and rocked my baby in tranquility. Far from being singled out for a lesser experience because I am a breastfeeding mother, I lingered in the refuge created just for me.

Friend, whatever form motherhood takes for you— conception or adoption; stay-at-home, work-from-home, or work-outside-the-home; going it alone or surrounded by support—yours is a journey of deep spiritual value. The spiritual life *is not* only for those with the freedom to sit quietly and meditate, but also for those of us who are called away to continue giving deeply of ourselves.

REDEMPTION IN PRACTICE

Breathe

Even at our most overwhelmed and exhausted, we breathe. Every few seconds we receive the air of life into our bodies . . . and release. For a moment we rest, suspended and surrendered, in the space between. And then we repeat—again, and again, and again. This cycle is never broken, awake or asleep, stressed or at peace, happy or sad, for as long as we live.

This is the starting point, the place in which we begin to see our daily cycles and tasks as spiritual disciplines. By taking a moment to listen to the sound of our own breath, we quiet ourselves. Try this: Breathe in slowly and deeply— then hold for a second. Breathe out slowly and completely— then observe that moment between breaths. In the space of a few minutes try to think only of inhaling, exhaling, and rest. As your mind begins to wander, gently return it to your breathing.

It is one thing to do this while sitting quietly alone and

another while you're chasing kids down the grocery-store aisle. Our goal is not to be mindful of *every* breath, but of *some* breath. Try at first to notice your breathing once during the day, and over time it will develop into a habit. Post notes in your house, car, or phone, reminding yourself to *just breathe.* Inhale deeply and realize you are breathing in God's unfailing love. Exhale and release into his unceasing presence.

Suddenly, breathing—your easiest daily accomplishment—is an act of worship, meditation, and prayer.

PRACTICE

- *Be aware.* As often as you remember, consciously notice the rise and fall of your breathing.
- *Be intentional.* Once you are aware, intentionally inhale deeply, hold for a moment, and exhale completely. Take a moment to experience the pause between breaths.
- *Worship through breathing.* As you breathe deeply, consider with gratitude the life God's Spirit has placed in your body, his presence in this very moment, and the peace his love provides. Choose a one-word prayer to whisper to him in your heart as you exhale.

The Spirit of God has made me;
  the breath of the Almighty gives me life.
JOB 33:4

12

Walk

Moms walk everywhere: up the stairs to get a diaper, down the stairs to do the laundry, into the other room to pick up the crying baby, through the department-store aisles, to the park so the kids can play. Without adding anything to our daily list, the walking we do can become a spiritual practice.

As you walk, try to notice the feel of the ground as your feet touch the floor. Hard wood, cool tile, soft carpet, dew-drenched grass. Whether you're walking barefoot or clad in boots, notice the way your feet meet the ground and push off again.

This awareness literally grounds us to our present place and moment—I am *here*, and I am here *now*. This same here and now is where God meets us, and this grounding allows us to stay present in his peace. As we focus on feeling the floor beneath our feet, each footstep can become a prayer.

Remember that God's love is the foundation we walk on, as sure and inescapable as the gravity that holds us in place. Of course, this will be harder to remember when you're walking toward a food fight or rescuing a toddler from toilet diving, but leave reminders for yourself around the house that when you walk, you walk in God's presence.

PRACTICE

- *Be aware.* As often as you can, take note of your steps, the ground beneath you, the muscles and movement of your feet. Realize that you are *here*. Stay present in this place.

• *Go slowly.* Unless there is a real emergency or you're running for the joy of it, don't rush. Take the time to experience the moment and day you are living: For better or worse, once it passes, it will be gone.

• *Remember the foundation.* God's love surrounds us: "In him we live and move and have our being" (Acts 17:28). And this includes walking. As you take the steps each day requires, remember that you are grounded upon the solid rock.

For in him we live and move and have our being.
ACTS 17:28

———————— *Be* ————————

It happens every time we moms step foot outside the house—someone implores us to cherish every moment with our children. We can't go anywhere without hearing, "Enjoy them while they're young! It goes too fast." The more appalling our children are that day, the more likely we are to be bombarded by this conversation. Cherishing every moment is easier said than done during a tantrum at Target. The whole idea becomes one more sure sign of failure.

It, too, seems like a ridiculous demand when we're in the thick of 24-7 caregiving shifts. The key to seeing motherhood as a spiritual discipline, however, is cultivating the ability to stay present in our daily tasks, to reap value from our actual circumstances. How can we do this after weeks of sleepless nights, when we've nearly lost sight of ourselves and any sense of perspective?

As with each of these practices, start where you're at—and start small. The goal is not one long victorious day of cherishing, but one single moment of awareness in the midst of all that's going on.

Does your baby look adorable when he triumphantly wrestles the teething ring into his mouth? Is the sun reflecting off your toddler's soft hair? Does your daughter's face light up as she describes her schoolyard adventures? For one second, just one moment, let go of all that burden of stress and exhaustion, and stay in that place. Experience it fully, recording it into your consciousness. Let your gaze rest on what is in front of you—your precocious child, the brilliant sky, or the powerful emotion. Whether the moment is a blessing or a challenge, realize that right now, *right now*, you are alive. You haven't always been and you won't always be, but right now you are *here*, in God's presence.

For just a moment, dip your toes into the water and experience *being*.

PRACTICE

- *One moment.* Instead of a goal that will result in a longer "didn't do it right" list, aim for one moment in your day when you are present in your body and with the people around you. In the midst of a busy day, use your breathing and walking exercises to quiet yourself and arrive in the present.

- *Notice the little things.* The sound of your child's voice, the softness of his new skin, the strength of her growing body. These are the moments we don't want to miss, and they can trigger us from the chaos in our heads and hearts and into the present.
- *Rejoice in the gift of being.* These little things in life point us to a profound reason to rejoice: In this moment we have life and breath. These are gifts from God, and it is in him and through him and to him that we exist. Even in the dark days, there is this blessing—and for a moment we can grasp on and hold it. Offer a word of praise and thanksgiving to the Giver of all things.

From him and through him and for him are all things.
To him be the glory forever! Amen.

ROMANS 11:36

CHAPTER 2

CONSECRATION

She Carried God under Her Heart

IT BECKONS TO ME, THIS QUIET SACRED SPACE. "The Convent of the Blessed Virgin Mary" reads the arched sign above the door. There's precious little peace and quiet in a mother's life, but here I am, standing unexpectedly at the entrance to this chapel. The open doors draw me in. I don't even try to resist.

Once inside I take a deep breath, desperate for life. My spirit wills my body to relax, my mind to leave thoughts of shopping lists and toddler discipline at the door. I take it all in, accept the invitation, and welcome the surprise of solace. Protestant that I am, I fumble uncertainly with the holy water at the doorway. I'm so grateful for this gift of sacred space, I don't even know how to approach it.

I begin to walk through the gorgeous, empty room. My

senses are bombarded in a totally different way than normal. No cacophony of children, no piles of work to do, no phone beeping and twitching in my back pocket. Instead, light and color, candles and incense, tapestries and stained glass. The bread and the wine. The loaves and the fishes.

As I walk, I study the stained-glass windows—each one in order, leading to the next, telling a story. The first shows the angel Gabriel appearing to Mary, telling her she has been chosen of God, explaining what is to come. The most unexpected of surprise pregnancies. Yet Mary responds with surrender and submission: "I am the servant of the Lord; let it be to me according to your word" (Luke 1:38, ESV). This grips me powerfully, from one pregnant woman to another. We have so little control over our lives, over the things we hold dear. Everything irrevocably changes over a few drops of monthly blood—or the lack of it. Our task is to listen, wait, and accept—to surrender. In the hidden womb of the spirit this is the beginning, or the end, of everything.

In the second window, Mary holds the newborn baby Jesus. What isn't depicted in the sharp lines of the glass is the extended story, but I can readily fill in the details. The hours that came before the serenity. The knife-edge between life and death, the blood and the water. What an astonishing thought: This messiest of human moments is when God breathed his first breath.

Then, the third window. Mary and Joseph finally find their son who ran off, unbeknownst to them, to teach in the Temple. I see in her face the anxiety, relief, bafflement. My spirit cries out with the realization of the task now ahead—giving up, letting go, humbly realizing that this child is no longer primarily an experience of her own, but a person and identity all *his* own. This baby may have begun as part of her body, literally one person with herself, but now he will forever be somewhat of a mystery, somehow inaccessible. Though the rest of us mothers have never and will never give birth to the incarnate Word, we, too, must learn each day to *see* our children, without defining them. To let go without abandoning. To say, "Your life is not about me but about yourself and what God is doing in you and who he has created you to be." For Mary, and for all of us mamas everywhere, the profound experiences of motherhood give birth to a new soul—and then we must begin to fade into the background. But we treasure up all these things in our hearts.

At the fourth window I'm stopped in my tracks. Mary, watching her son on the cross. The look on her face is easily recognizable. She confronts a mother's ultimate fear—the pain and suffering of her child, the breaking of the body and life she so carefully built and nurtured. The God-man mocked, put on trial, carrying a cross, stumbling, dying. Mary watching, watching and weeping. She cannot know the redemption that lies ahead—only that this is her son who learned to walk clutching the hem of her dress.

Entranced by these stories of color and glass I find myself near the altar, standing before a life-sized statue of Mary. She holds her baby, Jesus, who reaches for her face. Joseph stands at her shoulder, protecting them both. They seem close enough to touch, real enough to encounter. I wait, transfixed, trying to understand what it's all about. Such a familiar scene—the *most* familiar scene—man, woman, child. A family. Mary, looking so much like the mother, wife, and woman she is . . . with God playing on her lap.

I am struck by the scandalous, beautiful wonder of it all. Mary, Joseph, and Jesus. The everyday intimacy of family. The real-life, flesh-and-blood quality of God's work in us: his birth, life, and death. Translated to us only inside the language of our own birth, life, and death. God's most powerful acts, his Incarnation and redemption, did not break out of these most human of actions and identities—but rather worked *within* them.

For the first time, I look upon God's work through the eyes of a mother.

Mother of God

Here, where I least expected to find her, I encountered the child-raising spiritual hero I had sought. She isn't known for charity work, words of wisdom, or tranquil demeanor. All nativity scenes to the contrary, she probably looked just as beleaguered walking through the door of Joseph's carpenter shop as I would have. Yet we have honored and revered her for thousands of years, simply for submitting faithfully to the task and title given her: *mother of God.*

The convent's images drove into my heart a message that has never stopped resounding. Mary and Jesus will never be duplicated, but what strikes me is how ordinary it all seems. The Messiah she carried, God-made-man, was unlike any other—but his redemptive acts were communicated through the common, everyday vernacular of our bodies. From the confusing, exciting, terrifying news that she had conceived, to the agony and ecstasy of birth, through the years of wondering and worrying, to the moment she wept as she held her son's dead and broken body in her arms.

Can I imagine what it means for a woman to give life to the Son of God? *Never.*

Can I wrap my mind around the fact that the acts of pregnancy, labor, nighttime feedings, and skinned-knee-kissing are the same doorways God walked through to enter the world? *Not hardly.*

All at once I see the two stories I know so deeply, side by side. The gospel story my soul has been drinking in since cradle roll next to the story my adult body has inhabited for a decade. Conception and birth, training up a child, then letting go—alongside the good news of Creation and Christ, body and blood, bread and wine. Unexpectedly, motherhood becomes the purest window I have to see that when God touched mankind most dramatically—when he walked among us and redeemed us—he did not do so with the supernatural moves of a superhero or mythological god like we were expecting. He used the same life seasons given to each one of us. To reveal himself he came to earth not on a bolt of lightning or on a cloud, but carried in a womb, born of a woman, knitted into flesh and blood—incarnated. To redeem us, this same human body did not triumph majestically but was broken, his flesh torn, his blood spilt—death.

Surrender, and birth. Surrender again, and death. So very, very physical. So absolutely *creaturely*. These are the bookends of our lives, the entrance and the exit, experienced by all, escaped by none. And God's redemption played out within them, among them, and through them.

This means that the sacred does not float ethereally beyond the reach of mortals. The sacred has mingled inseparably with the mundane.

Body and Soul

Born and raised on American evangelicalism, I "asked Jesus into my heart" at least a hundred times. This clichéd metaphor expresses a spiritual reality, and we too easily forget there is more here than symbolism. Jesus spiritually alive in my allegorical heart is one thing; the King of Creation cutting baby teeth and going through puberty is something else. Do we actually believe what we proclaim: that God took on flesh and walked among us, with all the humanity that entails?

While I metaphorically have Jesus *in* my heart, Mary physically carried God *under* her heart for nine exhausting months. She labored and pushed, pouring out water and blood and risking her life to give God his first breath. She rocked him to sleep, nursed him from swollen breasts, and sheltered him with the softness of her body. She cut up his food. She placed tiny pieces of fish in his hands and taught

God-made-boy to take and eat them. The wine she poured out for him, the bread she broke for him.

These were not acts of salvation, but of ordinary living. And yet, in the hands of God they became the stuff of Incarnation and redemption.

We easily relegate God to the intangible, imagining him hovering over the starry skies but missing him in the faces of our neighbors and the rhythm of our routines. It's much easier to believe we could connect to the sacred through meditation than through scrubbing bathroom floors. We sort our lives into two buckets—the physical, bodily, and tangible over here; the spiritual, sacred, and intangible over there. But why?

The answer, at least in part, goes back thousands of years to the ancient teachers. Plato, a Greek philosopher who lived four hundred years before Jesus, saw the spiritual world as more real than the earthly world, which was an illusion, a shadow of the real thing. Saint Augustine, a church bishop who lived about four hundred years after Jesus, weaved these ideas into his own writings, intertwining them with Christian thought.

This idea colored certain traditions of Christian faith for centuries, offering little use for the physical world of creation—including our bodies and their functions. As many saw it, the body simply impeded the soul's journey and should be suppressed as much as survival allowed. The "fully God" aspects of Jesus were much more compelling than the "fully man."

The Protestant Reformers wove much of this into their own doctrines and traditions, so in a way our discomfort with the unity and value of body and soul is a family tradition.

Like Christmas carols and fruitcake recipes, the suspicion that our bodies cannot be a way to God has been passed down through generations of Catholics and Protestants alike. Spirituality is a way to escape, rather than celebrate, our flesh—or so it seems.

But this is the brainchild of Plato and the Greeks, not of Jesus and the Hebrews. If we dig deeper into our Christian ancestry, we find a very different stream of thought that has also flourished from the beginning. The early church fathers were enamored by the Incarnation—that God actually and literally became part of his creation. Believing Jesus to be fully God and fully man, they considered the birth of God the ultimate cosmic, world-shattering event. They emphasized that in taking on human form, Jesus united the physical and material with the divine. In accepting our skin, birth, life, and death, he blessed these mortal things and made them somehow immortal, holy, and sacred. In becoming part of his creation he made perfect his creation. Not only as a man but as an infant, as a child. As he made his way—fully God and fully boy—through these busy, fleeting days of youth, he brought divine presence and blessing to every stage of human existence.

And as we'll see later, the Creator who called his handiwork "good" has shown a tremendous tenacity to nurture it. The good news proclaimed in the Bible from beginning to end has never been that God will get our souls out of this earthly mess, but that he is in the process of redeeming it all—bodies and souls alike.

The miracle is not that Jesus was a human (we see humans every day) or even that he was God. The biblical, Christian miracle is that he was both God *and* man, divinity fully embodied in flesh and blood. God, connected to his mother by an umbilical cord and passing through the birth canal. The creator of the universe sinking small hands in the muddy ground, dribbling sand from his mouth, getting food in his hair. Trailing after Mary and Joseph, followed in turn by brothers and sisters, running off with friends. He learned to read, to pray, to care for the household animals and do his chores. God himself did these things and more. He did not despise or belittle them—he embraced and blessed them.

If, in becoming human, God somehow blessed the very act of being human, isn't it possible that in all these daily acts of living he left a sacred residue as well?

———

That morning at The Convent of the Blessed Virgin Mary, I stepped away from the chaos of my daily life, looking for solace in a silent, sacred room. And yet I found that, in its very act of pointing me to God, the blessed story launched me back into my own life.

The beckoning my heart heard is not to run off into seclusion, shrouding myself in prayers and candles until I find him—as much as I would enjoy that, and as true a calling as it is for some women. No, for mothers and householders everywhere, the beckoning is to go back into the flesh-and-blood world of crumbs in the car seat and missed-nap tantrums—and find him there.

Right where he met us in the first place.

CONSECRATION IN PRACTICE

Eating and Drinking

Even moms need food eventually, whether we're grabbing a bite between music lessons and baseball practice or sitting down at the table with the whole family. Physical nourishment cannot be avoided. And so, this cyclical need provides excellent soil for spiritual nourishment.

But between airplane spoons and school-day reports, it's easy to consume without thinking, without awareness that eating is a holy act of life-giving. Beneath our rituals and recipes is an indisputable fact: We eat to sustain our lives, and we do so by consuming other life. Plant or animal, every useful thing we take into our bodies (toddlers, I'm sorry, but sand, stuffed animals, and plastic rings are not nutritionally useful) was once part of something alive. Through eating, this other life gives life and health to our own bodies. What an amazing relationship and privilege—the life and death of another becoming life for ourselves.

Our bodies give off signals about food all day: *Time to eat!* or *That smells good!* or *Enough!* Allow these signals to prompt your spirit as well. When your tummy growls, reflect for a moment that even as your body craves that juicy burger or chocolate bar, so your spirit craves the presence of its Creator. Both sets of desires are real and necessary. Open your heart to him, even as you fulfill your physical needs.

When you are comfortably filled, take a deep breath and experience contentment. Mealtimes can be rushed or routine, but they still hold potential for delight, feasting, celebration of a need met, and gratitude. Our daily bread sits before us, provided by God's blessing and our own hard work. We have enough for another day, and this is no small thing.

Remember that this is practice, not perfection! Even if you remember to try this for only one bite, at one meal, one day a week, you will be creating a new spiritual discipline in your physical routines.

I'm eating a plum as I write this, my teeth sinking through taut skin and soft fruit as juice dribbles into my mouth and down my chin. My children are munching on plums of their own, and I'm sure this will result in a few stained T-shirts. Yet somehow this is a beautiful moment of worship: the joy of eating mindfully.

PRACTICE

- *Reflect on the miracle of life.* Consider the holy act of life giving life as you receive physical nourishment for another day.

- *Taste it.* Depending on the stage of your kids, lingering over your meal may not be an option. In fact, some of our most chaotic moments are at mealtimes! But try to place at least one bite intentionally, mindfully into your mouth and *taste* it. Observe the texture and flavor of the food, the temperature and refreshment of the drink. Be present with the physical and spiritual process, even if only for a moment.

- *Express gratitude.* Think about the many hands and hours of labor that brought this food from farm to table. Express thanksgiving to God, as well as to whomever prepared and served your meal, and to those at the table with you.

Taste and see that the LORD is good.
PSALM 34:8

Cooking

If receiving food can be a spiritual practice, why not cooking? The physical task of providing nourishment for another's physical body is also deeply spiritual.

Some people love to cook. If you are one of those magical creatures, the process of creating an artful, healthy meal may already be a worshipful expression. Others (like myself!) find daily kitchen tasks to be an unrelenting burden. Wherever you fall on the love it–hate it spectrum, children need to eat, and most moms bear at least some of the responsibility for making that happen. Between shopping and planning, food prep, serving, and cleaning up, feeding our families can easily fill what little time we have.

Service is a powerful component of the spiritual life, and in the tasks of food preparation, we serve our families in a vital and fundamental way. Without continued sustenance, no living creature can grow and thrive. In providing meals, we don't merely cross another task off the list; we contribute powerfully to the building of a life and body. Serving someone in so visceral of a way is inherently spiritual. After all, Jesus told his disciples that when they offered food to someone who was hungry, they were offering food to Jesus himself (Matthew 25:34-40).

Not only is cooking for a hungry family an act of service, it is also an opportunity to remember the presence of God. The methodical, linear motions of cooking can calm and order our thoughts. Even while we're being pelted by Cheerios and questions about sea monsters, the familiar rhythms of chopping and stirring build a framework on which we can focus our hands and minds solidly in the present—noise, chaos, attitudes, and all. Unlike some tasks, the tactile nature of working the ingredients with your hands invites this—and the danger of dinner burning on the stove insists upon it!

PRACTICE

- *Reflect on the miracle of life.* As you prepare food for your family, reflect that this meal is a life-giving gift. Though it may appear mundane, this work is absolutely vital to life. Your hands have become vessels of God's continued creation in the bodies of your offspring.

- *Be mindful.* Notice the food that passes through your fingers, whatever it may be: flour, salt, beans, rice, vegetables, fruit, meat, fish. Feel its texture and temperature, the weight of former life and the potential life it holds. Consider where these ingredients came from and the powerful role each will play in sustaining your family.

- *Consider the loved ones you serve.* They may be clinging to your legs or wiggling against your back while you chop veggies, but even without enough peace and quiet to form the words, allow the chopping of your knife and the stirring of the wooden spoon to be a prayer of blessing over them.

I will be fully satisfied as with the richest of foods;
with singing lips my mouth will praise you.
PSALM 63:5

Household Tasks

Kids create unending piles of dishes, toys, laundry, and mess of all kinds. Eventually, they will tend to these things for themselves (and for you!), but that day can seem like a long way off. Whether you spend your daylight hours at home or in the office, moms have plenty of housework to top off their to-do lists. It can be easy to lose ourselves in the piles of dirty dishes.

There is a circular pattern to these tasks that render them never-ending. No sooner have the floors been scrubbed than mud and grass are tracked in through the front door. Once one load of clothes is folded and put away, another pile of spaghetti-and-grass-stained pants has formed on the laundry room floor.

Before you get too discouraged, did you know there are ancient spiritual practices that see the repetitive nature of these tasks as a blessed opportunity for meditation? The Benedictine order, for example, intentionally places household tasks within the spiritual routine, naming "work" alongside "prayer" and "reading" in the daily disciplines.[2]

The key to turning your workload into a spiritual discipline lies in attitude and focus. Rather than hurrying mindlessly through a project, pay close attention to it. Feel the plate in your hands as you wipe it clean; intentionally set it aside and reach for the next. Notice the texture of the fabrics as you fold one small shirt after another. Experience the circular muscle movements as you scrub the bathtub or counter; watch as the grime yields to clean.

As with any of our tasks, the difficulty is not in *seeing* them as meditative, but in maintaining this view while children call from the toilet or empty the snack cupboard. And yet, the aim in any meditation is to practice being present during distraction.

Yes, my sister, without even paying the fees to attend a

meditation retreat, you, too, can practice the meditation of household tasks. Emptying the dishwasher as a spiritual discipline—who knew? Receive this challenge as an opportunity, not a burden. If a dirty carpet yields even a moment of spiritual fruit, accept it and rejoice. Notice and celebrate the winning moments, and spend no time nursing guilt over the rushed, impatient moments.

PRACTICE

- *Don't rush.* It's tempting to hurry through the piles, but there's another one right behind it. Whether you're washing the dishes, doing the laundry, sorting papers, or cleaning floors, work slowly enough to feel the things you're touching and experience your body at work.
- *Keep your mind on the task.* By their nature, these chores aren't rocket science. Our minds aren't required, so they scurry off. While our hands wipe down counters, our heads are making shopping lists, creating ideas and worries, rewriting past conversations. Gently train your mind to return to the present moment. You may find this needs to be done over and over again. But keep at it. After all, it is in *this* moment where God meets us—not in the past or the future.
- *See the value.* Rather than feeling that this is merely "stuff management," reflect that without such menial tasks, life does not move forward. The pursuit of

cleanliness is simply part of being alive. As you work, consider that these cycles of clean to dirty to clean need not be a source of discouragement, but a reflection of life's blessings. Then, offer a prayer of thanksgiving.

Whatever you do, work at it with all your heart, as working for the Lord.

COLOSSIANS 3:23

CHAPTER 3

CREATION

With the Help of God I Created a Man!

THERE'S A BOOK THAT BEGINS, "In the beginning, God created. . . ." I can't help but wonder about the prequel, the story forever lost to time. What happened *before*? What decisions and reasons, planning and research did it take for God to come to the precipice of creation—and leap?

My husband and I had been married for only a few years when we began peering into the murky tunnel of fertility before us. Should we enter? It was so dark, so impenetrable. The future gave up none of its secrets. Our current path—two adults, two jobs, no kids, time for work and play—seemed so much more controlled and predictable by contrast. What would the journey hold if we rushed ahead, and where would it lead? There was no way to know if this harrowing path would end in the greatest pains or the greatest joys of life—or both.

How on earth does anyone ever *decide* to create? How can something so weighty, eternal, and sacred include, however minutely, a *decision* deliberated by mere mortals like us?

And yet, the call to create is deafening. Our bodies and souls are tuned to the siren song, a rhythm marked by our own biology. Reproduction—whether physical or spiritual—is a holy task of being alive. Creation is a sacred center of being female.

And so, cautiously, recklessly, he and I held hands and stepped off the cliff.

———

The sun isn't up yet, but I'm awake. *Let's get this over with*, I think. I stumble out of bed and to the bathroom, right to the pregnancy test I opened and left ready the night before. Still half asleep, I am already so weary of this monthly morning ritual. Clear signs of on-time ovulation, carefully scheduled rendezvous with my husband, and missed periods notwithstanding, my hopeful early-morning questions are always answered with one line instead of two: not pregnant.

After several confusing repetitions, I visited my obstetrician. It appeared, he said, that conception was occurring but not pregnancy. The strong, delicate, all-important egg and sperm were cooperating long enough to delay my periods for a week or more, but not long enough to produce the hormones needed for implantation and a positive test result. Based on my history, there was good reason to expect this pattern to continue.

That was last week, but I am ten days late and need to know, again, for sure. So I cast this vulnerable question into the universe one more time. For the required two minutes I sit, waiting but not hoping. Before tossing yet another negative test in the trash I glance at it and feel the universe tilt: two bars.

Two pink bars.

I glance again, then stare. Then sit and stare some more. I walk over to the bed and wake my sleeping husband. "I'm pregnant," I mumble, befuddled, handing him the evidence. I'll never forget his sleepy eyes growing larger and larger and larger.

For the rest of the day I walk around in a fog of wonder, carrying within me a tremendous, unbelievable secret: *There is something new.* Whatever may come, good or bad, in this moment, *in this very moment*, my own tiny child is beginning.

Creating a new person isn't easy work, to say the least. This is the most difficult mission I have ever accepted. I don't dare leave the house without ginger ale and an arsenal of snacks. I dream of sleeping around the clock (in a carefully constructed nest of support pillows), but I get up and go to work instead.

I worry. I wonder. I eat more vegetables than ever before.

For weeks I am astonished. Everything in my life stretches and changes daily, making room for this new reality, this brand-new thing that changes *everything*. A new person exists. Somewhere deep within me is someone too small to see, without face or body or limbs, yet already containing everything necessary to become himself. Someone whom one day I will know and love as deeply as I know and love myself. This person both *is*, yet *is not*: he is *becoming*—inside of me.

Astonishing.

As the months pass, my child and my astonishment both grow, and I must expand to contain each of them. We see the heartbeat on the ultrasound. I am struck dumb, realizing my body is on loan; a helpless person has taken refuge in me to live and grow. Enthralled by the fully formed bodies of passing strangers, I find myself thinking, *Look at your ears! Your hands! Your eyes! It worked! It turned out okay! How did that happen?* Observing people make reckless choices, I swallow back shouts of "Do you know how hard your mother worked to give you this precious body and life?"

Friends beam at me affectionately and reminisce, "When I was pregnant with Olivia . . ." With a shock I realize that someday I will look at a person I know by heart and say, "When I was pregnant with you . . ."

He *has* put these astonishing treasures into jars of clay. A million of my tiny decisions and chance happenings have colluded and, by God's sovereignty, resulted in *creation*. Someone brand-new has begun, and we—mortal man and woman—have set it in motion. God has placed the tools of creation into our own trembling hands.

More specifically, into my womb.

Today I am creating new life.

Genesis

I have good company in this astounding task. A ribbon laces around me, and you, connecting us to a great line of matriarchs. Beginning with our mothers and grandmothers, it weaves its way back to the very dawn of time. And then, leaping even beyond the boundaries of existence, this ribbon finds its spool in the sacred space before time began. For in the beginning was God.

And creation is one of God's signature moves.

The opening chapter of the Bible is a beautiful song. It tells of a loving, rejoicing, intimate Creator who purposely fashioned the universe for himself. The song teaches that the foundation of reality is *relationship* between this Creator and all he has made—that we are not merely nature but *creation*. That our lives are intentionally fashioned with purpose, hope, and possibility. God created. God proclaimed his creation "good."

On the seventh day, the work of universe knitting was complete, and the outcome was glorious. The song ends with the Creator resting from his labors. Can you imagine the Lord's satisfaction as he looked upon all he had made—and then, amazingly, rested here among us? The seventh-day "rest" implies not simply exhaustion after much effort, but a king "coming to rest" in the place where he will dwell and reign.

In other words, what our Maker made is not only a good home for his creation, but *for himself as well*. This is key to the beautiful, subversive story—God is not only deity, but *Creator*. We are not merely nature, but *creation*. He has proclaimed the work of his hands to be good and is relationally present among us in a permanent, ongoing sense.

In Genesis 2, the tone changes from song to story. In a dry, dusty desert we meet the main character, the Gardener, who personally forms a man by hand from the dust of the ground and breathes his own life-breath into his lungs. The Gardener then sows his garden and gives it to the man to care for, both plant and animal.

God, of course, is the Gardener, who remains passionately involved in the nurture of the garden and its creatures. He walks among them and talks intimately to them. This story highlights the same message sung in the opening poem: Nature is not only material—an equation of atoms and cells—but *creation*. Intimately, lovingly, purposely formed by an intimate, loving, purposeful Creator.

The human pair have a job to do. They are to work the garden and care for it. Together, they become his creation assistants.

And Eve—whose name means *the mother of all living things*—is pregnant.

———

Can you imagine the first pregnancy?

Each of my three pregnancies was unique and amazing, but

the *first* has a way of searing your soul. Storks delivering softly swaddled babies has nothing on the incredible facts of reality. My body became ground zero for a miracle. New life formed within my belly; a new soul was woven from the nourishment of my blood. This is the stuff of magic, of fairy tales—yet in pregnancy the unbelievable becomes tangible in my flesh and bone. In our first pregnancy, we discover that this preposterous story is *true*, happening literally in our midst.

Miracles don't get more up close than this.

How much more *wonder*-full must the very first pregnancy have seemed to mother Eve? Where once there were two, now here were three. When once creation sprang from the hand and mouth of God, now he used the love of husband and wife, the blood and womb of a woman, to call forth someone entirely new.

Then, with all her strength and courage required, came the pain and dangers of labor. Eve hung in the balance between life and death until, in exhaustion and wonder, she held this first infant in her arms and declared with astonishment, "With the help of the LORD I have brought forth a man" (Genesis 4:1).

And so it has always been. And so it will always be.

The first time we mamas learn there is new life forming within us, we can find it impossible to believe. Who can imagine the reality of tiny fists clenching or lips sucking? Even during the months of kicked spines and trampled bladders we can barely hold the idea of a brand-new child in our minds. We watch as elbows protrude through our tightened skin, but still we don't really believe it.

Yet pregnancy and birth are the most commonplace experiences. Each man, woman, and child is conceived and born. Every puppy, zebra, and dolphin is created and birthed in flesh, water, and blood. We see it every day, all around us, everywhere we look. Still, creation hits us like the staggering mystery it is.

Sisters, we are made with this capacity and calling—to receive, to form, to create. God's creative power orchestrates through our female bodies and souls. He has chosen us. We are given a spectacular mission, coming alongside the Creator in this most privileged, astonishing of tasks.

God imagined and formed these bodies of ours with so much care and love from the dust. He created our frames in his image and pronounced them "good." He crafted the beautiful and strong miracles of male and female, conception, pregnancy, and childbirth. All the blue skies and crashing oceans, towering mountains and tangled trees, helpless babies and exhausted parents—he made every piece. He created intimately, on purpose, with love. And then he asked us to continue creating, one new life at a time. The siren song to create that I hear in my every cell is the song he composed in Genesis 1. Because the good news is that he will continue creating and redeeming this world until he has made it right and new.

And in his sovereignty he has requested my partnership. Our help, my sister.

With the help of God, I have created life.

Breath of God

I creep silently into the dark room, hand on the doorknob, not chancing any noise. Slinking across the carpet, I risk waking my sleeping daughter in order to behold this great wonder: the gentle rising and falling of her chest as she breathes. Placing my hand on her sleeper-clad belly, I let myself relax into the waves of her peaceful body.

It is this breath we listen for in the first seconds after birth, this same breath we cling to in the final end-of-life vigil. And it is this breath we mamas watch so closely all the days between. Rising and falling, in and out, ebb and flow. The rhythm that tells us all is well. This is the essential breath of life.

The beautiful poem of creation in the book of Genesis has a character we often overlook: the Spirit of God. This Spirit— or *ruach* in Hebrew—means wind, or breath. Grammatically, *ruach* is feminine. Especially in poetic passages depicting his creative power, the language of God's Spirit or breath often evokes the feminine qualities and activities of the Creator.

In the first two verses of Genesis, God—in Hebrew the grammatically masculine *Elohim*—is about to begin creating. Meanwhile, *Ruach* is hovering over the waters. Can you imagine it? That silent moment before all begins, and God's breath of life is ready. *Elohim* about to command, *Ruach* hovering as a mother bird prepared to receive and shelter her soon-born offspring. These metaphoric images are deeply evocative of the moment of creation.

This image of divine breath appears again and again throughout Scripture, marking God's power to create and sustain life. In the story of the Flood, when God unmakes and remakes the earth, it is the *ruach* (breath) of earthly life that is destroyed (Genesis 6:17). Later, it is God's *ruach* (wind) that comes again to hover over the waters of chaos, once more pushing them back to bring forth new life.

The wisdom literature of Job and Psalms also contains poetry describing God's creative power. These words, spoken through God himself, ask:

> *Where were you when I laid the earth's foundation?*
> *Tell me, if you understand.*
> *Who marked off its dimensions? Surely you know!*
> *Who stretched a measuring line across it?*
> *On what were its footings set,*
> *or who laid its cornerstone—*
> *while the morning stars sang together*
> *and all the angels shouted for joy?*
>
> *Who shut up the sea behind doors*
> *when it burst forth from the womb,*
> *when I made the clouds its garment?*
> JOB 38:4-9

Here in the midst of the morning stars singing and the sea bursting forth is the *ruach* of God—the wind, breath, spirit that gives life. Job declares in 12:10 that "in his hand is the life of every creature and the breath [*ruach*] of all mankind." Then again in 33:4, Job proclaims that "the Spirit of God has made me; the breath [*ruach*] of the Almighty gives me life."

The Psalms also contain a creation poem:

> *The LORD wraps himself in light as with a garment;*
> *he stretches out the heavens like a tent*
> *and lays the beams of his upper chambers on their*
> *waters.*
> *He makes the clouds his chariot*
> *and rides on the wings of the wind.*
> *He makes winds his messengers,*
> *flames of fire his servants.*
>
> *He set the earth on its foundations;*
> *it can never be moved.*

PSALM 104:2-5

Through the rest of the chapter, the psalmist continues describing the many creatures the Lord has made: "When you take away their breath [*ruach*], they die and return to the dust. When you send your Spirit [*ruach*], they are created" (Psalm 104:29-30).

God's creative, life-giving power is nearly always *ruach*—his breath or spirit. *Ruach* is the essence, the divine gift that transforms the dead into life. The sacred Breath that gives breath. *Ruach*, hovering over the birth-waters of chaos, surrounding the embryonic earth. *Ruach*, pouring forth new life when all was destroyed by the second birth-waters of the flood. *Ruach*, sent from God Almighty to create and make alive all creatures of the earth.

Our Creator God gave to Eve's strong and beautiful body a piece of his creative power. And though God is neither male nor female, in the stories and poems that tell of his creative authority, the Hebrew words and depictions are feminine.

And so, during the exhausting, all-encompassing season of pregnancy, we are doing God-work. Creation is one of God's signature moves. And by his grace, creation is one of our signature moves too.

It is audacious, this partnership between the Creator and me. Especially audacious during these final weeks of pregnancy as I appear to grow by the minute. People around me are startled and alarmed by my size, the thoughtful (pained) expression on my face, and the slow, awkward waddle of my gait. Instead of saying "How adorable you look!" and "Can I touch?" they now say things like "Any time now, huh?" and "Are you okay? Are you sure? Do you need me to call an ambulance?"

After one such exchange, the concerned gentleman paused, then reflected, "This must be an amazing experience for you."

Yes. Yes, it is. Literally the experience of a lifetime.

My thoughts are consumed with nesting now, always focused on the practical. Creation is nothing if not practical.

What will we name him? How many more things do we need to buy? How will we afford all this? Have we filled out the insurance forms? We need to interview pediatricians. Time to eat again. Time to go to the bathroom again. What is labor going to be like? I'm tired. This hurts. I can't walk anymore. I need to sit down. Oh, those are my ribs you're kicking! I can't breathe. I just dropped my wallet on the floor, and there is no way I can get down there to retrieve it.

These are the months of my life most consumed by the physical, my body and its needs filling my every thought and decision every moment of the day and night. Yet the physical practicalities in this season of creation are deeply spiritual— as is the life-giving culmination coming so soon.

This nine-month spiritual practice, having taken over our entire bodies and selves, begins to sink deeply into our souls. Whether or not we mamas find time and energy to contemplate this mystical, spiritual, physical act of God that has overtaken us, the impact is there. The doing is enough, for now.

We are learning. We are being changed. Our minds concentrate on lifting each foot and setting it down without too much pain, but our souls are being taught. With every cramped-lung breath we take, *ruach* pours God's living Spirit through our beings, deep into the secret place where his hands touch the dust of our bodies and form new creation—itself waiting to receive the sacred *ruach* of God.

Any day now.

CREATION IN PRACTICE

Menstruation

Blood is the essential element of our bodies. It represents both life and death, and a mother's body holds both these together in constant tension. Nowhere do we live this more vividly than in our menstrual cycle.

The advent of our monthly periods can be challenging, filled with emotional and physical pain. Discomfort and tiredness make our daily responsibilities more difficult to meet. Some of us feel dirty, "cursed" by this bloody ritual, ashamed and worried that someone might see—or God forbid, smell—our situation. Can these most physical of days be a path to God, a spiritual discipline?

Through recorded history, women's bodies were viewed as powerfully mysterious: like the moon and the tide we ebb and flow, and in the midst of it all we create and harbor new life. The essence of life and death mingle in our bodily cycles and in the blood that flows from our wombs. This mystery—and the blood—was inexplicable, so often considered unclean.

Yet these physical rhythms were intentionally placed within us by our Creator. The cycle may not hold the magic powers of a mythical moon goddess, but neither is it undignified or dirty. The menstrual cycle is a beautiful, powerful process of life-giving that the Creator formed with his hands, placed into our bodies, and joyfully pronounced "good." God has not cursed his daughters; he has empowered us.

Starting a period means, to some degree, *loss*—of blood and hormonal momentum, sometimes even of hope and new life. For many women this is an inescapable reminder of infertility and pain. For most of us it brings darkened emotions.

Our society worships the pursuit of happiness, and this plunge into monthly difficulty *does* seem like a curse. Yet pain, loss, and darkness are a true part of our lives, and there is value in a period of lament and struggle each month.

God has given women amazing diversity in the seasons and cycles of just one month—a time for anticipation, a time for loss, a time for purpose. When we learn to be present with our bodies, paying as much attention to our internal schedules as we do our daily calendars, we pay homage to our Creator and the wonderful, mysterious, diverse creatures he has called us to be.

PRACTICE

- *Set aside time for Sabbath.* There is a rest time signified by the start of our periods—a break from sexual activity and less energy for extra work. As possible, view these days as a signal for rest and reflection. Burn a special candle to prompt your senses to remember that these are days set apart, given by God.

- *Pay attention to your body.* Get to know the ebbs and flows of your entire cycle. When do you feel tired, and when are you energized? Is there a week when you feel gorgeous and sexual and another when you would rather curl up alone in sweats? On what days do you feel light and free or anxious and depressed? Whatever each day and week of your cycle brings—be it hope or despair, energy or exhaustion—pay attention. Stay present right where you're at.

- *Lament and let go.* Monthly blood means so many things. For some it means infertility, the loss of hope, the loss of tiny life. On an emotional and hormonal level, this is a time of releasing and starting over. Emotions are easily at the surface, so process your fears, anger, or grief as they come. Allow yourself to dive into this season of letting go, and gather the strength to begin again.

There is a time for everything,
  and a season for every activity under the heavens.
ECCLESIASTES 3:1

_____ *Sex* _____

Many of us probably have some difficulty imagining sex as a spiritually formative endeavor. For so many reasons, sex can be complicated, especially for exhausted moms desperate for space. More so if your past or present relationships were or are painful or damaging. Sex has often been viewed as a necessary evil, something we must capitulate to for the sake of reproduction but too base or deceptively pleasurable to be wholeheartedly embraced. Alternatively, it can be seen as nothing more than the casual fulfillment of hunger, a basic need and human right but nothing more.

Yet both of these extremes fail to remember that sexuality is *central* to the physical, created world—and to the creative process. Male and female united in physical, emotional pleasure and service to each other—God *made* this in the Garden. He proclaimed this *good*. This union creates not only a strong bond in marriage, but brings forth children, families, and a future. How can God be repulsed by one of the most basic and central components of what he lovingly, intentionally devised?

Sex is a powerful and fundamental human expression, given to us by God. Healthy, respectful, marital sex abounds with the sacred. In this merging of physical, emotional, and spiritual communion we serve and are served; we give and receive at our most vulnerable yet powerful places. Sex can usher us—and allow us to usher our spouse—into intimacy, beauty, and joy. And occasionally, in the midst of it all, we create a new human soul.

However grotesquely humankind may have warped this good gift—and in so many ways, we have—sexuality remains, at its core, a good and perfect gift. We are not required to choose between being physical, earthly creatures and being spiritual children of God. He formed us to be both, together, in the same sexual body.[2]

PRACTICE

- *Enjoy.* The starting place to viewing sexuality as a spiritual discipline is to relax and be present in the experience. Whether you love your sex life or struggle from guilt, shame, or exhaustion, allow yourself to be present in whatever the experience is for you. As you are able, become aware of your body and your relationship. Notice the intimacy, the emotional and physical pleasures. Focus your attention on the union being formed between yourself and your husband.
- *Give.* Sexuality, when it is healthy and respectful, can be a deeply profound site of mutual service and submission. In a positive, loving sexual encounter, each partner can approach the other inside a paradox of vulnerability and power, longing both to give and to receive, to simultaneously enamor and be enamored. This is a deeply spiritual posture of humility, vulnerability, and the willingness both to give and humbly receive.
- *Reflect.* Our deep sexual longings and the transcendent experience of sexual union have always been

---

[2] If you are not in a safe, mutually respectful relationship, please know that God does not condone sexual abuse. If your sexual relationship is painful for you and your partner is unable or unwilling to listen, please find a trusted female leader at your church or medical/counseling center who can help you.

metaphors for our longings for God and the joy of his presence. As you enjoy this physical, emotional, relational gift, reflect on our Creator's good plan for building community and calling forth new life—all while realizing our longing for him.

Let him kiss me with the kisses of his mouth—
for your love is more delightful than wine.

SONG OF SONGS 1:2

Awakening

We've all had our share of sleepless nights, but on most days we do awaken from a night's rest. Perhaps it's an alarm, a crying baby, or a before-school snuggle that announces the new day. Few of us moms have the margin to begin with a "quiet time," but it is still possible to use the opening moments of the day to set the tone. This is a sacred time, a time between times, when creation is reborn and God's mercies are new.

However you receive your wake-up call—whether you have ten quiet minutes or only ten blurry seconds, whether you're a morning person who thrives in the early hours or a night person not yet fully awake—begin by reaching out a hand to God. You might want to literally reach your hands to him. Or perhaps lie silently in bed for a moment, resting in his presence. Or have a prayer ready, a simple, "Lord, I live and breathe in you today," to set your heart and mind on him from the very beginning.

Does this mean we'll soar among the clouds all day? Not

hardly! The blown-out diapers, sick kids, forgotten home-work, and work meetings will bombard us soon enough. But through it all, we will be going about our day *in him*. And before our eyes are fully open, we have a chance to set this in stone.

PRACTICE

- *Remember.* As with so many of these practices, the biggest hurdle is just remembering. Place a note, a small piece of art, or something beautiful by your bed to remind you that you are awakening in the beauty of God's presence.
- *Pray.* Even if you have only the time it takes to open your eyes and sit up, use these first silent seconds to center your heart and mind. Have a short prayer ready in your memory or on a notecard, and begin by giving the day to Jesus.
- *Be still.* In this quiet moment, simply be still, breathing deeply, lifting yourself to the Creator. He already knows every blessing and trial the day holds. He will walk beside you.

Let the morning bring me word of your unfailing love,
for I have put my trust in you.
Show me the way I should go,
for to you I entrust my life.
PSALM 143:8

CHAPTER 4

INCARNATION

Flowing with Milk and Honey

IN THE MIDDLE OF THE NIGHT, my water breaks. It gushes everywhere, surprising me, flooding me in every possible way. These months of creating this precious child climax suddenly with urgency, danger, and hope. My body takes the lead, bossing all of us around—husband, baby, and me. It has grown used to being dictator over the past months. My womb will have its way no matter what.

Just in time, we arrive at the hospital. *This is it. This is really happening.* None of us will leave this building the way we came. We will be entirely changed.

Still dripping amniotic fluid, and now sweat and tears, we arrive in a room called "the birthing room." Aptly named, because birthing is done here—paradoxically named, because this place has the exact opposite qualities of birth. It is clean, sanitized of every possible bacterium, designed to limit risk and maintain control. And I, in the throes of labor, am bursting with life and possibility, with uncontrollable, unforeseeable dangers, opportunity, and chance. I need the safety this sterile room offers, but I do not miss the irony. In this room intentionally stripped of life, life will burst forth and take its first breath.

We Americans have an infatuation with *sterile*. It means "free from living organisms" and "thoroughly clean." So we put sanitizer on our hands and spray chemicals throughout our house. We expect dinner to come with disposable cutlery sealed in plastic bags. To our minds, life can only thrive in the supposed shelter of *sterile*.

But sterile also means "uncreative, unfruitful, and infertile."

Life is the exact opposite of sterile.

Teeming is what we are, we human creatures, we mothers. *Tactile and palpable.* And never so much so as in these harrowing moments of labor. In this well-scrubbed, highly monitored birthing room I have brought a cacophony of uncontrollable life—and it is bursting out all over. Nearly every imaginable bodily fluid passes between my legs in the making and birthing of this new soul. Every undignified posture, uncivilized position, and unspeakable sound is present on this endless night.

Then, red and wrinkled, still slick with water and blood, already howling in protest, he is placed on my chest. Soon milk will begin to drip from my swollen nipples. All the mess of the whole world, it seems, is present in this business, breaking forth into this clean, white, beeping room full of well-scrubbed strangers. But we, the baby and I, overflow this pristine space with something entirely new and extraordinary.

We are bursting at the seams with *life*.

Incarnation

At the most celebrated of birth stories, Mary's delivery room was not so hygienic. This sacred, holy day was crowded with noise, blood, animals, and chaos. The morning dawned with a man and a woman sleeping on the hard ground after days of traveling on foot. Can you imagine how she looked and felt, walking? One hand supporting her bulging belly, each step jostling a painful elbow into her spine. God-made-man's head against her bladder. Nothing brings on contractions like walking, and she has walked so far.

By the time they reach Bethlehem, the contractions have made this mother both exhausted and alert, her husband urgent and resolute. The fragrant, moldy hay and straw of the stable is itself crawling with life, but it is soft and warm. More than sufficient for a birthing bed. Among the warm bodies of sheep and donkeys, Mary labors and delivers. God is born among us. The Word becomes flesh and makes his dwelling on earth—surrounded by all the flies and mites and animals and *life*.

The sacred hour of Incarnation.

Incarnation means "embodied in the flesh." When Jesus was knit together in Mary's womb he was *bodied*. He took on flesh and blood and bone with all our complicated earthiness.

Central to Christianity is the conviction that our spirits and bodies are connected—that what happens to our bodies matters. We believe, proclaim, and practice that the God who made bodies took on a body and meets us still today in our bodies. We declare that the God who made the physical earth visited it in the flesh and is still entirely committed to nurturing his creation. Our good news is that, in the end, this Creator-God will not separate our souls from our bodies or his presence from the earth. For after his body was broken in death, he did not meet us in spirit but in *resurrection*. As the firstfruits of the new creation, Jesus is both our Savior and our future promise. God will not abandon but *redeem* our earth and bodies. He will make his permanent dwelling with us in the restored and recreated heavenly city on earth.

In other words, there is no escaping this good, physical world he made. He came *here*, and it is *here* he will return. Our God is incarnated. Our hope is embodied.

And who has a front-row seat to our bodies—in their creation, incarnation, and nurture—if not mothers? Who is the midwife of God's presence in our bodies if not mama?

———

There is a website that pokes fun at the idea that motherhood, if done correctly, can be clean and peaceful and orderly. The tagline says, "Relax on your pristine white couch and enjoy these realistic depictions of motherhood."³ These well-intended photos show happy parents with happy children, everyone dressed in clean, unwrinkled, white clothes (no stains or spills!), sitting on immaculate light-colored furniture (no Cheerio crumbs or juice box disasters!), doing everything with happy togetherness and great satisfaction (no tempers or chaos or rush!). I've spent hours howling with laughter at these captioned pictures that poke fun at the marketing actually used by other publications.

These stock-photography mothers glow, are always patient, and clearly have all the time in the world to care for themselves. And why not? Their children are well behaved and orderly, and the mess of life never gets in the way. Motherhood, for them, is immaculate ease. They can lounge on their clean white furniture in their clean, white, unwrinkled semiformal wear while their perfect children politely exist.

But, as this parody website masterfully demonstrates, we real mamas cannot. These photos are spotless and shiny, but they are sterile. They are "entirely clean," lifeless, and barren. Motherhood is the opposite. *Life* is the opposite. Life is full of *life*: our bodies, emotions, and souls bumping against other bodies, emotions, and souls in the most beautiful and ugly of ways. We are hungry, our hair is oily, our hands are dirty. We are creatures surrounded by creation. We are alive. We are creative and fruitful and fertile.

Mothers are the opposite of sterile.

Spirituality, too, is often mistaken for something that can

and should be pristine and spotless. We think of "spiritual" as peaceful and silent, pure and untarnished, having something to do with our emotions and thoughts and nothing at all to do with our bodies.

Bodies are unpredictable and messy—especially mothers' bodies! We flow with blood, milk, and fluids of all sorts. Our shirts are covered in spit up and our hands in baby poop. We make peanut-butter-and-jelly sandwiches, chop apples, and mop up spilled orange juice. We explore earthworms, scrub grass stains, and make mud pies. We brush tangled hair and gently scrub our children's skin while they splash and holler in the water.

Motherhood is loud, not peaceful—messy, not clean. And certainly never spotless.

Remember when we learned about the stubbornly persistent misunderstanding that bodies and noise and mess are what we must escape to seek God, find him, please him? While these ancient ideas are debated in seminaries and churches, we mamas battle them unconsciously in our bodies, families, and homes. Because if spirituality keeps the spirit and discards the body, what hope does a mother have?

This one misconception takes the beautiful miracle of creation and life—and the mysterious, demanding, exhausting role we mothers play within it—and transforms the miracle into shameful drudgery. Motherhood is seen as, at best, a necessary evil that should be taken care of as quickly and discretely as possible (to make time for more important pursuits) and by the least important people (to free the valuable members of society for more sacred goals). Mothers, and their tasks, are looked down upon. In the spirit of equality, we are encouraged to try to find a way to be both: a mother and also important; a mother and also productive; a mother and also spiritual. It seems inconceivable that motherhood alone could embody it all.

Yet the cultivation of spiritual fruit, like the birth of our children, is hands-on, tactile, and real. Motherhood *is* deeply physical—and deeply spiritual.

Skin-on-Skin Sacraments

My toddler raises my shirt as I pay for the groceries, peeking and groping: *Is the milk still there?* Shamelessly my preschoolers demand I wipe their noses and bottoms. Why else am I here, if not to serve their bodies with my body? It's as if we still share one self, are still connected by an unseen cord. Not a single hour passes without one of them unabashedly needing my physical self in some way.

This is my backstage pass to their strong, beautiful, growing bodies.

Children are hungry for action. Who cares about sentiment! I sit down and they pile on me, each outdoing the other for the most bodily contact. They bury me in an avalanche of faces, mouths, heads, arms, legs, tummies, and bottoms, all pressed against mine, all wiggling. Each physical need beckons us to *know*, to taste and see, to make contact, to touch. These tiny creatures are designed to lull us into mingling our bodies with theirs, to getting our hands dirty with them each and every day. Because this is how we fall in love. Up to our elbows in childhood, we can *know* these enchanting, exasperating creatures.

As my children understand and teach me every day, a deep level of knowing is born from these daily rituals of touch, from knowing someone or something in a tactile, mundane sort of way. We wrap our newborns close to our chests, both of us unclothed, "skin on skin." My ten-year-old son grabs my hand and forgets to let go. On a chemical level we bond, weaving bodies, hearts, and minds together in deep communion as we follow the week's routine. These are intimate acts of knowing, the way we learn another human creature.

We mamas hurry to hide leaking breasts behind nursing pads and blankets. But from their very first heartbeats, children need their mothers to flow with milk and honey.

————

The people of this village are very poor—you can hardly even imagine it. They have no running water, no electric lights. They have clay jars and water wells, oil lamps and wicks. Their dirt-floor homes house large families and household animals. These people work hard from dawn to dusk, with their hands and their backs, to keep life and limb and family intact for another day.

A famous man is in town, a spiritual teacher and healer. He is so holy, they say he comes from God. And this teacher, this spiritual man sent from God, is not a stranger. He is one of them.

You might expect someone so wise and renowned to be elsewhere, discussing lofty ideas in an ivory tower with others of his caliber. But he is not. This man is here.

He is standing down by the lake, leaning against a boat full of fish on a hot day. He is talking to fishermen and the women washing clothes in the shallows. With feet already caked in layers of sweat, dust, and mud, he's getting his hands dirty. The hem of his coat is soaked with sandy brown water and who knows what else.

The Son of God makes no effort at all to set himself apart from the rabble of daily life. He sits among the running, screaming children and steps into the putrid fishing boat.

The elite and powerful of the village are disgusted. *This should be below him*, they say, shaking their heads in repulsion and walking away.

But Jesus' words are not hard to follow—even, and yet especially, for this uneducated, working-class crowd. His stories are of sheep, fish, bread, and water. He announces the kingdom of heaven by describing farming fields, seeds, coins, and oil lamps, by discussing vineyards and servants, wine and weddings.

His friends are laborers. They get up each day and work hard to create another day of life for their families, then go to bed exhausted. Never does he belittle them or prod them to dream bigger, to think loftier. He is God, but he is man— and poor, nearly homeless, not royalty or upper class. Jesus of Nazareth is so entirely *one of them* they can hardly find anything special about him at all. He fits right in with the messy busyness of everyday life.

And it is here, in their midst, with their routines of fish and wine and bread, that he proclaims the kingdom of heaven.

The gospel, Jesus teaches, is in the yeast, as a woman kneads it with her bare hands into the cool, pungent dough. It is in the soil, so warm and moist when freshly turned by muscular arms and backs. It is in the tiny seeds of mustard and wheat, painstakingly saved and dried from last season's harvest. Each one is so easily dropped or lost as it floats through the sower's fingers, yet each one holds an entire promise of future life and sustenance.

Jesus places the gospel in these tactile things, with all the grit of life surrounding him, because it is through all this touching, tasting, and smelling that his own sheep— his beloved, hardworking, human flock—*know*. And it is through these most mundane, touchable, smellable, tasteable pieces of commonplace existence that he shows them, and us, to find God and know him.

Jesus delivered the good news in a rough, messy, hands-on package of donkeys and dusty roads, bleeding women and lepers, water from the well, and wine from the water. Holy work in the world has always been like this: messy, earthy, physical, touchable. God created these things, every one of them. Jesus joined us in the flesh, with all that entails— womb and breast, childhood and adulthood. Even death.

Especially death. He left something of himself in the water and oil, in the bread and the wine. This is how he taught us to find him.

There has never been any other way.

Even today, we know God best through our fingers and lips. The holy sacraments are tactile, elemental stuff. We are reborn in the waters of baptism and blessed with drops of holy water. Oil is set aside for anointing and blessing. The bread of his body crumbles in the upheld hands of the minister while the cup of his blood is poured out. These are the elements that bring us into the presence of God, that are sacred and hallowed, that draw our focus unto the very essence of the Lord's redemptive power. We declare that within these everyday words and ingredients resides a sacred grace, a consecrated moment touched by God. But they are also the most basic building blocks of life, the physical elements that sustain our creaturely selves—especially those ancient laborers in whose midst these rituals were born. Water. Oil. Bread. Wine.

After my children's bath, I have been more than sprinkled with water: doused is more like it. The food that feeds my family crumbles through my hands too, all day, every day. The milk that comes from my breasts is the nectar of life for my babies.

If Jesus taught fishermen and their wives about the Kingdom using fish and bread—and if we have met him ever since in the water and the wine—could it be that the ingredients of my own ever-repeating chores hold a sacred grace?

I've been known to knead bread, drink wine, hold a slippery, scaly fish just caught from the river. I have held a tiny seed in the palm of my hand and turned over the warm, dark soil. I have sorted out the weeds from the fruit.

But mostly, these days, I cut peanut-butter sandwiches into triangles and carrots into sticks. I wash urine-drenched Spiderman sheets and beloved Hello Kitty blankets. I sort math homework, third-grade chapter books, and spelling tests. These are the tactile experiences of my own mundane chores. If Jesus were to spend the day in my village, I think he'd be sitting among the dust bunnies, unopened sale flyers, and cookie crumbs of my living-room floor, saying, "The kingdom of heaven is like a worn-out shoe a child found in the bottom of his backpack." And then he'd teach me how to find God's truth right where I'm at.

Is it possible that, in the wonder of creation and Incarnation and the life-giving routines we are always acting out, we pass through sacraments—are covered in, coated in, up to our elbows in sacraments—every day?

Perhaps there are a million stories about lost library books, mismatched socks, sliced grapes, and unrinsed sippy cups that begin with, "The kingdom of heaven is like a mother, who . . ."

———

My body will never forget the force of that final push— the pressure, the screaming, the release and relief as a newly minted person slipped from my womb and into the hands waiting to catch him. The way his arms and legs stiffened and eyes scrunched—his entire body shocked by the bright, cold, traumatic entrance into life.

What words are sufficient to describe those amazing, amazing moments? Exhausted, broken and torn, I am delivered of a baby. It is over. But more so, it has just begun. He has begun, is here, on my chest. I look at him, touch him, hear his cry. Everything changes: the world, my heart, my life. Three times I have lived this day.

The cord—so stiff and blue and cord-like, looking so not-human yet made and used and now ejected by my body, the last physical thread connecting him to me—will soon be severed. In my body the two of us—my husband and I—became one. Now, in the cutting of this cord from my body, the one becomes three.

Incarnated, embodied life begins all over again.

INCARNATION IN PRACTICE

Body

It is a powerful feeling to hold your child's body in your arms, their compact selves radiating vitality. Every square inch of a child's frame is a spectacular thing, a wondrous miracle. We marvel at how small yet strong they are, how innocent yet tenacious. Just a few years ago, these bodies did not exist at all, yet now they run through the grass and holler our names in the dark. These bodies summon our awe.

Mothers, we are not known for rejoicing in our own bodies. We're often ashamed of how we look, hiding behind the camera to avoid confronting a permanent record of our appearance. But why? Stretch marks, baby fat, and gravity have nothing on the miraculous tasks our bodies perform. Our babies are made and nourished here; our children take refuge here.

Our frames, too, were formed in the secret place by the Creator. Our culture may worship youth and an immature idea of beauty, but our mother-bodies are breathtaking and gorgeous. Whether we got our children by birth or adoption, they find in our flesh and muscle the safest, most sacred place on earth.

Each day is filled with bodily needs—needs of our family but also of ourselves. In loving our bodies we perform a holy act of service toward God's creation, caring for our own little corner of what he made and pronounced good. Our bodies are worthy of our respect, admiration, and care, as an act of service—with worship and gratitude to God.

PRACTICE

- *Celebrate your body.* Stand naked in front of the mirror, not with a critical eye, but rejoicing in the strong and beautiful form God has made. Touch your stomach gently and intentionally, not roughly or dismissively. Look at your body and don't be afraid.

Speak kindly: Don't demean yourself by pointing out saggy tummy muscles or extra baby fat. Instead, speak of the miracle God fashioned in the adult female—we can love a man, create and birth a child, live to tell about it, heal, and do it again! Imagine! We can find the strength to wake four times a night with the baby and still rise at dawn with the preschooler. So touch, look, and speak reverently.

- *Care for your body.* With such a long line of people requiring our services—children, husbands, parents, siblings, in-laws, neighbors, friends, coworkers—we women often put ourselves last. And though we must meet these responsibilities, we'll do so best if we're not crumbling. When you feed your family, feed yourself too. When your family rests, allow yourself to rest. Drink a tall glass of water, thanking God for life. When possible, remember that self-care for Mom is a service to everyone.

- *Enjoy your body.* The amazing gift of a strong body is ours for a limited time only, so enjoy it! Does running or exercise energize you? Stay present with your muscles as they move with strength, your lungs and heart as they rise to the challenge. Do you enjoy beautiful things? Celebrate the splendor God has placed in you without guilt or shame. Do you love physical touch? Pay attention to your fingers as you touch the people and things around you. Notice these sensations with gratitude.

*Do you not know that your bodies are temples of the
Holy Spirit, who is in you, whom you have received
from God? You are not your own; you were bought at
a price. Therefore honor God with your bodies.*

1 CORINTHIANS 6:19-20

Breastfeeding

When we mothers breastfeed our children, we physically portray a great truth: Sacrifice and beauty often intermingle into
one. We nurse our babies, literally feeding our children from
our own bodies. We pour forth our time, body, and soul for
the survival of another person, in a process that is painful,
joyful, bonding, and demanding. This powerful mix impacts
our spirits.

Breastfeeding is a difficult sacrifice, and it is not possible for everyone. It means physical pain, difficult latches,
plugged ducts. It means howling infants too angry to latch
on. It means getting up in the middle of the night again and
again. And again. It means a tether connects mother to baby
that cannot be severed even for a short time. It means that,
while others can take a turn, *mama* is irreplaceable; the buck
stops only here. Nursing mothers can only leave for so long
and only go so far. The twin pains of an empty tummy and
full breasts will certainly bring us back to our infants. Mother
and baby need each other for relief in perfect synergy.

So much of our time, so much of our bodies, is given
through breastfeeding. As I once overheard someone say,

breast milk is free only to the extent that a mother's time and body are not valuable. Breast milk is extremely costly.

But this sacrifice contains great joy. There is deep bonding in the hormones, emotions, decisions, and physicality of breastfeeding. Each of those hours is given and received. Each drop of milk binds two people together, as life flows literally from mother to child. It is beautiful, joyful, and good. And it is deeply spiritual—in all its forms. As I learned firsthand, there are countless reasons why a mother might need to choose bottle over breast. If that is your situation, these practices are still for you. As we cradle our babies in the rituals of bottle-feeding (and prepping or pumping, washing and boiling), our bodies and souls are equally given over to the pouring out of life.

PRACTICE

- *Stay present.* Use the stillness of nursing to awaken yourself to the present. Turn off the electronics, at least some of the time. Focus on your baby's noises and movements, and store them deeply inside your heart. Allow the hormones released during letdown to quiet your own mind and soul. Reflect on your thoughts and emotions. Sort through them, offering them to God. Allow the stillness to usher you into a time of worship or prayer. Quiet yourself as you quiet your child.
- *Give and receive.* Outside the womb, is there a more extreme example of gift-giving than breastfeeding? Consider the wonder of it: Your body is mysteriously connected to your child's, producing the nutrients,

comfort, and physical touch she needs to thrive and grow. As we nurse, we are poured out, emptied for the sake of another. As you feel your breasts empty and your baby relax, acknowledge the life-giving gift you have poured out. Then, open your spirit to the Creator, and allow his Spirit to fill you.

• *Rejoice.* This most physical of actions is profoundly spiritual. Enjoy the intimacy and mutual relief. Give thanks for new life, for bounty, and for nurture. Delight in this time with your child, in the dawning hours of his life. And in those in-between moments, those soaked-nursing-bra-and-damp-T-shirt moments, rejoice that you are dripping with sacrament, with the God-given nectar of life.

Yet you are he who took me from the womb;
  you made me trust you at my mother's breasts.
PSALM 22:9, ESV

Water

Water has always been considered deeply powerful, as both a physical and a spiritual element. And no wonder—no living thing can survive even a matter of days without it. We are formed in a bag of waters. Even as adults we are more water than any other physical thing. Water *is* sacred to our physical life.

And to our spiritual life, too. Water has been considered

spiritually purifying since ancient times. Bathing in a holy river, rebirth in the ritual of baptism, and the blessings of sprinkled holy water are universal expressions of spiritual cleansing and renewal. Even nonreligious folks find crashing ocean waves, mirror-still lakes, and gurgling streams spiritually soothing and life-giving.

We moms are doused in water every day, from sippy cups to dishwater to bath time. We take muddy children, sticky floors, and stained socks—and renew them. Moms are dripping with the sacrament of water: the liquid our toddler dumps on the floor or spits up into our hair or splashes across the bathroom. The water that boils over on the stove because we've rushed to a crisis in the other room. The water that gushes out of us in the moments before birth. The water we use to soothe a feverish forehead. The suds that wrinkle our hands in the kitchen.

It is all the same stuff—that physically, spiritually life-giving liquid.

PRACTICE

- *Be aware.* As often as you can, notice the water that covers you each day. For example, instead of going through the motions of washing hands, reflect on the process of cleansing and the spiritual reality water reflects. Feel your inward spirit washed pure as the dirt runs from your fingers and palms. Thank God for the clean heart he has given you through his Son.
- *Service and blessing.* Pray over your children and

family as you care for them with water. As you fill
glasses, bathtubs, and sinks, reflect on the service you
are offering to God and the blessing of clean, life-
giving water. As you wash your household, envision
your spirits also being cleansed and renewed.

· *Relax and renew.* When you think of it, allow your
own cleansing time to renew your spirit and body
together. In the bath or shower, set aside worries and
plans for a moment and let the warm water do its job.
Take deep drinks of cool water and notice how your
body responds. Enjoy the relationship your body and
soul has with this sacred element. Use this time to
silently wait on God in prayer.

He leads me beside still waters.
  He restores my soul.
PSALM 23:2-3, ESV

CHAPTER 5

NURTURE

Made in the Image of God's Love

THE SUN ISN'T UP YET, but my children are. I am too now, awakening to small feet padding through the hall toward my room for their before-school snuggle. My children: inbound.

Before they arrive, my barely awakened consciousness bursts open with the unmistakable sounds of conflict gathering steam and about to erupt all over my sleepy bed. The growing urgency in their footsteps doesn't express desire for me so much as their resolve to win—there are three of them, and only two spots next to me. Three large creatures launch themselves into my sleeping space and vie for position: Elbows, knees, and shoulders jostle everywhere.

The idyllic morning cuddle is never in reality what it is in my head. With tempers shot before we've been awake a full minute, we give up and start breakfast. In an hour these big kids will be too busy with friends and school and games to even consider slowing down long enough to nestle close to me. Yet my desire—our desire—to maintain the innocence of pre-dawn sleepyheads keeps us coming back in our jammies for more each and every day. Tomorrow morning we'll be back, each of us longing for this soft heart-and-body nurturing.

But not too long ago, it was all snuggling . . .

———

Hour after hour, all stretches of the day and night find me right here, rocking and nursing. As I cradle my infant, I gaze out the window at the trees and sky that never seem to move. This strikes me since my life has slowed down in a similar way—previously busy days distilled into a seated position.

Rock. Nurse. Repeat.

Yet like the unmoving trees outside my window, this season of stillness contains work and growth, the deep nurture passing between my body and my child. The warmth, the milk, the love and belonging required to build this person from infant to toddler moves soundlessly from me to him. Hour after silent hour. Day after exhausted day. Night after sleepless night.

Who knew that sitting down could be so exhausting? Through the moments I cherish and the moments that chafe, I wonder, *Does this matter?*

Looking down at my baby, I am so aware—everything

I eat, drink, breathe, my every mood, word, belief, and emotion somehow make their way not only into my body and soul, but into his as well. We are mysteriously yet irrevocably linked, he and I. My choices impact not only myself but his life and well-being. There is nothing I do or think or create or say or feel that he will not soak up to some degree, through his genes or his tummy, his ears or his hands. This world will both nourish and pollute him—body, mind, and soul.

It all matters.

So these slow, invisible hours hold a sacred power we can only begin to glimpse. My babies will not remember these long, sacred days, the most intense season of bonding between them and me. But what their minds will not recall, their very selves will testify. It is no small thing we mamas do in these wee hours—whether rocking a babe or snuggle-wrestling them years later. Nurture is a basic need, and humans die without it.

So many of us mothers, especially in these silent, isolated seasons, struggle to answer, *Who am I now?* It is so easy to lose ourselves in the repetition of service that goes unnoticed and unthanked. But God has shown us what is good and what he requires of us—to do justice, to love mercy, to walk humbly (Micah 6:8). These spiritual practices are in full effect as we pour ourselves out to helpless, dependent, vulnerable children day and night. And though our existence may have shrunk into this isolated place and time, our humble tasks hold eternal significance.

Alone in this chair, unmoving from this house, I take

responsibility for another person's body and soul. It is a long day of small things, but nothing on earth has its beginning outside this hidden, holy space. Parents—mothers—embody life for our children. We are living statues of compassion, nurture, love, and grace. These gifts may be unseen and unvalued outside the world of blankets and teddy bears, but they are everything within it.

In the end, what we give will spill out of our house and into our communities, mingling with other offerings given by other mothers and fathers—and create an entire generation.

We are not performing great spiritual deeds before a great audience, but we are performing them nonetheless—before God and before our children and our own unfolding souls.

These thoughts flood my mind, sleeping baby still in my arms. *Oh little child, you have been entrusted to me, and your soul is more priceless and more awesome than my human mind can grasp. For my whole life I have longed, I have labored, to be a nourishing and not polluting place for you to thrive and grow.*

He wakens suddenly, disoriented, looking up at me sharply, quickly, as though to see where he is, whose arms he has been vulnerable within. His eyes meet mine, and he relaxes, falling again into my chest, safe and at peace. Asleep.

Under Her Wings

The Bible is full of imagery of God as a loving parent. In the New Testament especially, Jesus and the apostles proclaim and pray to God as Father. In one of Jesus' best-loved parables, God is understood as the lavishly loving, forgiving father of the insolent runaway son. Not only did this father forgive his son, he reestablished him back into the family; he *celebrated* him. The father was watching and waiting for him to come, extravagantly running down the road to meet him.

It may feel normal, after a few thousand years of reminders, to imagine God as a parent. But at one point it was a shocking new idea. If we stop and think about it, what an unbelievable reality! Can you imagine it? The awesome power and beauty that spoke creation into being, choosing to interact with us in the intimate terms of parent to child? Yet this is exactly what the Bible says. In description after description, God is portrayed not only as a father but also as a mother.

Do you remember that moment when a onesie-clad toddler first let go of the couch and stumbled toward you, proudly nailing a few shaky steps with a beaming face, then plopping on his diapered bottom? Have you felt the ironclad grip of a little fist wrapped around your index finger as that child toddles tentatively down the hall?

The prophet Hosea describes God as the one who taught his people to walk, taking them up in his arms, healing them, leading them with kindness and love: "When Israel was a child, I loved him. . . . It was I who taught Ephraim to walk, taking them by the arms. . . . To them I was like one who lifts a little child to the cheek, and I bent down to feed them" (Hosea 11:1, 3-4).

Through the prophet Isaiah, God says, "Can a woman

forget her nursing child, that she should have no compassion on the son of her womb? Even these may forget, yet I will not forget you" (Isaiah 49:15, ESV). Then in Isaiah 66:13 God declares, "As a mother comforts her child, so will I comfort you."

God is a mother hen longing to gather her chicks under her wings (Matthew 23:37 and Luke 13:34). He is a mother eagle that spreads her wings and hovers over her young, catching and carrying them as they learn how to fly (Deuteronomy 32:11-12). God is even described as the one who gave birth to his people (Deuteronomy 32:18).

Some scholars believe the name *El Shaddai* comes from the word *shadaim*, which means a woman's breasts or bosom.[4] In other words, he is the God who sustains and nurtures as a mother does.

Of course, God is neither male nor female, not physically mother or father any more than he is an eagle or hen. Yet the Scriptures lovingly, joyfully, powerfully express the creative, nurturing, faithful love and care of God in parenting language—again and again and again.

Steadfast

In one of my favorite passages of Scripture, God introduces himself.

Let that sink in for a moment. What better way to learn about God than by paying attention to what he says about himself? Though in one sense all of Scripture is God's introduction, in Exodus 34 God reveals himself to Moses. With these words he makes himself known to Israel:

The LORD, the LORD, the compassionate and gracious God, slow to anger, abounding in love and faithfulness, maintaining love to thousands, and forgiving wickedness, rebellion and sin.

EXODUS 34:6-7[5]

The ancient Hebrew word *hesed* ("steadfast love," the ESV tells us) is used twice in this passage—and 250 times in the Old Testament. It is *hesed* that God abounds with, and it is *hesed* he maintains to thousands. Scholars have called it the most significant Old Testament depiction of how God relates to his people. *Hesed* is a powerful, revolutionary idea, central to the biblical message. And this is personal, not just academic—*hesed* wants to turn your life upside down.

The beautiful concept doesn't translate well into English. Bible translators use phrases like *steadfast love* or *unfailing love* or *loving-kindness* or *compassion* or *mercy*. But the biblical word *hesed* goes further than any of these ideas. It means a love that cannot be shaken or changed or erased—no matter what you do or how terrible you are—because the love is not based upon you. It is based upon God. And remember, this is God talking. Talking about himself! By his own declaration this is God's character and identity, the foundation of reality.

Hesed love is like gravity. You can't get away from it. You can't change it. It simply *is*.

The Creator and Israel were not in a particularly lovey-dovey moment when God made this pronouncement. In fact, God had just finished entering into a covenant with Moses, only to discover that before the ink was dry, his newly covenanted people had built an idol and abandoned their half of the bargain. In the fallout of this betrayal Moses pleads with him, begging to see whom he is dealing with. God finally relents, hides Moses behind a rock for his own protection, and passes by. So in introducing himself with these words, at this time, the Creator powerfully demonstrates that his love and compassion for Israel is not based on their human identity or faithfulness—it is rooted in who *he* is, in *his* faithfulness.

This grace springs from the Lover himself and cannot be shaken or destroyed. Just as gravity does not pick and choose whom it will keep from spinning out into space, God's committed, steadfast love simply *is*.

Nothing has taught me about this sort of dedication more vividly than motherhood. The moment my child was first laid on my chest, something changed deep within me; there was no going back. We mamas ask no questions like, "Do I want to get up every two hours to care for this person who does nothing in return but scream and demand?" We simply do. We love, we give, we care. Perfectly? No, never! But again, and again, and again.

We must. It is who we are now that these children have arrived.

In response, our young ones blossom with love—but also with willfulness, stubbornness, conflict, and resistance. Just as humanity continues to hurl itself into danger and destruction despite God's loving care, so my deeply loved children deplete my patience and self-control *each and every day*. How many times have I told them not to leave last week's lunches rotting in their backpacks? Can they not see what happens when they sneak candy into their beds and leave it melting under the pillow? Could anything good come from yanking a book from a sibling who is peacefully reading?

Yet they do these things, and more, every day—and our love still abounds. If a scale exists to weigh the trouble our children cause us against the love we have for them, I have never seen it.

Let's read those descriptive words from Exodus 34 again. *Compassionate. Gracious. Slow to anger. Abounding in steadfast (hesed) love and faithfulness. Maintaining (hesed) love to thousands.*

Sound familiar?

These first words, *compassionate and gracious*, are most often used in the Bible to describe someone strong and powerful caring tenderly for someone who is weaker—like a parent with a child. And it is important that we don't miss this nuance. God's *hesed* love is not generic kindness or goodwill—it exists inside a covenant relationship of care between two people.

We often think of a covenant as a contract, but that doesn't really cover the power and beauty of the idea. A contract is an exchange of property: This is mine, and this is yours. I give you money, and in exchange you give me your car.

But in a covenant, there is an exchange of *selves*. The two people involved are *giving themselves to each other*. I am yours, and you are mine.

What better picture of *hesed* love do we see on earth than a mother with her young child? There is no legal paperwork needed to document the commitment because reality itself changed when this new person entered our lives. Birth certificates and adoption papers aside, we love because of our identity as mother-to-this-child. We mamas belong to our babies just as surely as our babies belong to us. We don't sign an agreement to sacrifice sleep and our social lives to care for our children—we nurture these creatures because we simply *must*. This is who we are now.

There was an irrevocable change in that birthing or adoption room. You belong to your children. They belong to you. You are bound together, and this cannot simply be undone. Our babies have done nothing to earn our love, but no matter how tired or exasperated they make us, we cannot simply stop loving and caring for them. This love has become our reality. It is our identity.

The Hebrews, encountering God so many thousands of years ago, considered this description God gave of himself as foundational. They understood reality as God in relationship with us like a mother with her child. I do not love my babies because they have earned it or deserve it, because they impress me or show real potential. I clip their toenails and play "this little piggy" to turn tears into laughter simply because *I am Mommy*. And they are mine.

Nothing can change that.

The nurturing actions of motherhood are not merely chores of drudgery that we'll eventually outgrow. In nurturing our children we walk in God's footsteps, just as we did in creating new life. We provide an icon, a picture of who he is, for all the world to see. Mothers are walking reminders that *hesed* love is the very foundation of the earth. In nurturing, we bear the image of God.

Living Icons

As we mere mortals go through the monotonous tasks of motherhood, we fulfill several important necessities at once. We provide for our children, who themselves are created, known, and valued by God. We step into a loving, nurturing role that is *at the very heart of who God is*. We mimic him, following in his footsteps, echoing his identity. And we create in ourselves a reflection of the gracious, compassionate, *hesed* love God rains down upon his people—regardless of who we are or what we have done, dependent only on who *he* is.

Do you see it? Cutting up avocado wedges for your toddler and a grilled cheese for your kindergartener. Hauling down the baskets of grass- and mud-stained laundry to wash before folding the last five loads. Waking up early enough to sign reading logs and drop the kids off at school before your own busy workday begins. Staying up late to listen to inexplicable tales of childhood anxieties. Stumbling toward the crying baby at 2:37 a.m. And 5:12 a.m. And 6:45 a.m.

These are not merely the list of chores we must do during

a particularly exhausting stage of life. This is the very stuff of God. This is *nurture*. Has bouncing a baby kept you from attending Bible study for a season? You are *living out* the Bible study in your daily motions and tasks. You may have lost the free time you once used to pursue God, but you are studying him *hands-on* through an intensive internship developed just for you. We mothers love our children with an imperfect, impatient, exhausted version of *hesed* loving-kindness, which gives and gives even if our children never reciprocate.

Because we simply must. This love is who we are now.

And in doing so, we practice the love and nurture of God. We are living icons of *hesed*, the most startling idea of all.

———

I have spent so very many worship services in the nursery. Or at home with the son who caught a fever his first week back to school. Or with a daughter who was up all night with the stomach flu. At first glance, these hours of isolated exertion feel like something lost, a delay in my chance to hear a sermon, worship with the body of Christ, and grow toward God. Another mile added to the ever-widening gap between "mother" and "society."

But they are so much more.

I know how isolating and lonely those hours can be, how very weary and depleted and invisible we feel when they stack up so high we cannot see over them.

But I also know that God did not describe himself as someone who arrives promptly to every church service or makes it to the office without ketchup on his jacket. No, God describes himself as *compassionate and gracious, slow to anger, abounding in steadfast love and forgiveness*—like a mother with her child. He describes himself as the father who eagerly waits for word from his son. As a gentle parent who teaches a baby how to walk, who leans down to feed and hold her. As the mother who gave birth and nursed her infant, who comforts and protects her child like a mother hen.

God is with the worshipers in the pew—the ones listening quietly as well as the ones wrestling crayons and graham crackers into the hands of noisy preschoolers. But he is also with those of us on the outside, and he identifies with us. These chores of child raising are not something to get out of the way so we can return to society's agenda, already in progress. Motherhood spirituality is not Plan B for those of us with no other choice, making the best of a bad situation. *What we do and who we are is foundational to the character of God.*

And so is the spirituality of these stressed-out, chaotic days.

Even if I manage to stay patient throughout the day, dinnertime gets me every time. Once more the peaceful, idyllic image evoked by the phrase *family dinner* is smashed into a million sticky crumbs of reality.

I leave the table just long enough to grab a drink refill but somehow long enough for the rumbling chaos to escalate toward full eruption. Returning, I find an entire box of cereal dumped on the floor—and two children sobbing. We weren't even having cereal for dinner. How did the box migrate from the cupboard to the table to the floor so quickly?

So the kids move from dinnertime antics to kitchen-chore antics, and I wisely escape into a different room to dodge the carnage of their cleaning. And one thing leads to another—bath time for little ones, showers for bigger ones. Bedtime stories for short attention spans, another chapter (or two . . . or three) of our current classic read-aloud to the others. And suddenly we find ourselves right back where we started the day: snuggling in bed.

Even now, even after all the wiggles and hollers have been spent, these little gnomes can't quite manage cuddle-standard. An elbow goes into someone's eye, the songs are interrupted, the prayer time punctuated by a somersault off the bed. I thought good moms had quiet, orderly children. I've even met some who do.

But sister, my bunch never does stop wiggling.

In the end, tossing them cups of water and kisses, I flee the scene.

Fifteen minutes later, though, they are asleep. I creep back in and stand there, just watching. Finally, now, it has arrived: the unbroken utopic moment when I simply look at them, kiss them, straighten their blankets without resulting bedlam.

Mothers, we are the source of all earthly comfort for these amazing creatures. And like all sources, we are rendered nearly invisible by our necessity. Do we notice (or thank) the air we breathe each moment? Does a fish understand (or appreciate) the composition of water? We simply *are*. We must be.

And though our precious babies will never remember the hours we spent rocking, the nights we spent nursing, the gentle touches and words we used to spin their childhood around them—though these memories will fade into the predawn darkness of their consciousness—*none of it is lost.* In nurturing our children, we are demonstrating for them the very image of God.

Take heart, mama. Then take a hot bath. And then, if you can, take a nap.

NURTURE IN PRACTICE

Cherish

Moms, we never stop caring for our little ones, do we? From the moment they're ours, we feel their needs as our own. We cherish them with emotions and words, but most of all with our actions.

Getting up in the middle of the night to nurse a hungry baby girl? Missing Christmas with extended family to stay home with a sick boy? Scrubbing every possible bodily fluid out of the carpet? Driving her to soccer practice and dropping him at a friend's house? We've got it covered. Moms are the Energizer bunnies of cherishing.

But the ceaselessness of hands-on demands can sow seeds of despair. Will we ever break free long enough to nurture something in ourselves? Is there enough margin to maintain our sense of self?

This season of pouring out *is* nurturing something in ourselves, if we can awaken to it. In this unceasing love and care, we most deeply reflect and echo—and see up close—God's own identity and posture toward us.

Cherishing our children, both emotionally and actively, is deeply formative to our spirits, for in doing these things, we grow close to the heart of God.

PRACTICE

- *Slow down.* Each day is so full, and there is rarely enough margin to do just one thing at a time. But when you can, even if just once a day (or week!), take a moment to *realize* the love you act out every minute of the day. Feel it. Reflect on it. Stay present with your child, and for just a second stay within the love you both need.

- *Reflect on God's steadfast love.* Remember that the love you feel and act on—imperfectly but consistently— is a reflection of the steadfast love of God. As you give faithfully to your children, thank him for *his* faithfulness and unending care. Reflect on the biblical imagery depicting God as a loving, nurturing parent. When you witness your children's vulnerability contrasted by your strength or experience a surge of love in the face of naughtiness, allow the truth of God's posture toward you, *his child*, to seep into your heart.

- *Don't get lost.* In all the caring for others, it can be easy for us moms to lose ourselves. It can even become a badge of pride: *I gave more than anyone!* But we can only really love our children—and our Creator—if we have an identity from which to give. The fact is, we *will* get lost at times. There will be days, weeks, or years when the giving drains us dry. But as fragments of your former self slough off, take note of the new self that emerges—and the new ways you reflect the loving faithfulness of God in the lives of your children.

Do not set your heart on what you will eat or drink; do not worry about it. . . . Do not be afraid, little flock, for your Father has been pleased to give you the kingdom.

LUKE 12:29, 32

Discipline

Disciplining my children has taught me about God's love like nothing else I've experienced. What a crazy cocktail of emotions flow when someone you love more than your life needs correction! Waves of love, anger, and grief crash down upon one another. We weigh short-term considerations with long-term strategies and past performances. We consider temperament, development, and heart. And then, with grace and truth, we do our best to teach our children how to follow the path of life. We hold them while they scream and sob.

And we maybe scream and sob a bit ourselves.

Teaching children about boundaries and consequences brings us up close and personal with grace, forgiveness, tough love, and unconditional love. As a mother I embody these heady theological ideas each day in my decisions and actions. These doctrines are no longer theoretical—they are part of who I am and impact everything I do now.

Is it possible to discipline intentionally and mindfully without taking these lessons into our own souls? We see ourselves—selfishness, willfulness, failure to rely on God—in our children's headstrong choices, but we also see God's steadfast love, grace, and mercy in our response. However angry we may start off, we don't want to destroy our children; we want to help them and teach them. We don't want to abandon our rebellious offspring. We want to restore them.

If this is true of us, in our weak and tired moments, must it not be perfectly true of God? We may not have much time to attend theology classes during motherhood, but we can study these truths of God in our children and ourselves on a daily basis.

PRACTICE

- *See yourself in your child.* Each time I hear myself shout, "I can't believe I have to tell you this again!"

I realize that I, too, require God's conviction about the same mistakes over and over again. As you discipline (hopefully with less shouting than I do), allow your own heart to be softened before God and your family.

- *See God in yourself.* It is all too easy to believe that God cannot really love us as we are. But consider your relationship to your children. Do you love them less when they mess up? The toddler in his twentieth time-out of the day drives us mad; the middle-of-the-night call from a teenager breaks our heart. But in both cases what we long for is a healthy relationship with a healthy child. God cannot possibly be a worse parent than we are—his grace and steadfast love are perfect. As you discipline, remember God's boundless mercy and grace toward you.

- *Rest in God.* After I discipline my young kids, I pull them into my lap for a "nest of love." Holding them tightly, I whisper, "Mommy loves you forever, Daddy loves you forever, God loves you forever. There is always enough love to make a nest of love." Can you offer this gift to yourself? Take advantage of the time-outs and lost allowances to open your hands, with your child if possible, to our loving Father. Accept his correction *and* his restoration with trusting, open hands.

Those whom I love I rebuke and discipline.

REVELATION 3:19

Sleep

Sleep is such a precious, sacred gift. Even when moms aren't getting any, sleep still takes up space in our thoughts and conversations. How can we get more? How are our babies doing at it? When will my toddler need a nap? When might I get a turn?

Sleep is sacred somehow. As we watch our children snore, we see how precious and vulnerable they are. Do we realize that we, too, shut down entirely for a time?

Similar to the experience of waking to a new day, the moments before we sleep can be a sacred time between times. As we soothe our children toward sleep, and while we settle ourselves down for the night, there are ways we can make this transition meditative and prayerful.

PRACTICE

- *Pray over your children.* As you rock your child or tuck him in, pray silently or aloud with words, songs, or your whole body. Perhaps choose a song based on worship or Scripture as a lullaby, or quietly read a favorite Scripture passage aloud. This intentional slowing comes at least once each day. Let's use it to recenter our spirits.
- *Reflect with gratitude.* As you go through your own bedtime routine, reflect on the events of the day. As you put away clothes and turn out the lights, consider what you can learn from the challenges of the day

(both good and bad ones). As you brush your teeth,
search your memory for the hidden gifts of the day
that went unnoticed in the hustle and bustle. As you
wash your face, bury the treasures you uncover deep
inside your heart and mind for safekeeping. Don't
spend time obsessing or rehashing; simply harvest
what is valuable and take it with you.

- *Rest in him.* As you lie down, end the day with a
  quiet prayer. This is not the time to go through a
  list of needs or bring heavy burdens to the Lord. Try
  something short and simple, like the Jesus Prayer:
  "Lord Jesus Christ, Son of God, have mercy on me."
  Simply end the day lying in his presence.

In peace I will lie down and sleep,
  for you alone, LORD,
  make me dwell in safety.

PSALM 4:8

CHAPTER 6

SERVICE AND SOLITUDE

All-Nighters with God

SLEEP WHEN THE BABY SLEEPS, they tell me. Wise words, but easier said than done. My one small hand nearly covers his entire swaddled body as I lie in bed, leaning toward him in the sidecar bassinet beside me. Too awestruck with the wonder of this new life, too flooded with postpartum hormones, too vigilant over this vulnerable soul to consider sleeping, ever. Whose eyes will watch this breathing miracle if mine are closed?

Sharing a body for nine months has left me incredulous. If an infant falls (asleep) and no one is there to hear him, does he make a sound? If no one is watching, does he still exist? I cannot believe this defenseless life continues if I am not awake to observe and enjoy it.

Sleep when the baby sleeps. In years to come I will answer back: What if your baby *doesn't* sleep, except in forty-five-minute increments, for months? What if your toddler wakes just when the baby nods off? Who cares for the big kids bothered by nightmares, wet beds, or sick tummies just as we've drifted off after the 2:00 a.m. feeding?

There are a million things keeping mothers from sleep.

However adorable the culprits might be, these years of sleep deprivation can decimate us. Where once there was a thriving, interesting human, now only rubble remains for future generations to dig through and contemplate. Sleep deprivation is, after all, an internationally condemned form of torture, designed to break even the hardest criminal or most devoted mother.

My heavy eyes watch this snoozing baby. His tiny head is slipping out of a hat that's much too big. Milk-blistered lips pucker into a serious pout, and long lashes curl against soft pink cheeks. Where did you come from, miracle child? And where does this love, this strength, to care for you every day spring from? How do parents wake up and begin again each day?

In these dark, wakeful times of service to my child, I experience such a deep sense of silence and solitude. In these wee hours the world sleeps, and only a few of us remain on watch.

And yet, during these midnight moments I realize so powerfully that I am not alone. Surrounded by a great cloud of witnesses, the weight of billions of mothers who have spent their nighttime hours in this way is palpable: We are united in these shadowy moments, rocking, pacing, bouncing, nursing, crying, worrying, wondering.

An even sweeter, closer presence is here with me as well. He, the Source of all life, has attended every one of these midnight vigils. He has joined every exhausted parent marking the passing of each nighttime hour. And he sees each of us. Even when *we* finally sleep, *he* stays vigilant. "Watch, O Lord, with those who wake, or watch, or weep tonight," prayed Saint Augustine, sixteen hundred years ago.[6]

Never before have I attended these dark hours so regularly, so I had no idea how palpable his presence could be in the moonlight stillness. God, the night watchman of the world, sitting in vigil, awake with every mother and child.

The Christian Practice of Service

We knew it was coming. The work, the responsibility, the obligations of raising children. But we can't prepare for something so massive. Motherhood requires every ounce we didn't know we had in us to give, twenty-four hours a day, seven days a week.

Too exhausted to think of anything besides placing one foot in front of the other (preferably with coffee in hand), we fail to notice the powerful spiritual forces encircling our constant service. Like a rich, life-giving fertilizer, our labors mix into the soil of our souls, enriching our spirits without our knowledge.

Service has always been a key component of the Christian life. Ever since Jesus took up the basin and towel, shocking his status-hopeful disciples with this undignified position, we followers have understood that he meant for us to do the same. Service slowly pries vanity and delusions of grandeur from our blistered hands, one humbling act at a time. It is difficult to become an egomaniac when an hour of each day is spent washing another's muddy footprints off the hallway floor. When Christians value service, they cultivate a spirit of giving and humility.

Richard Foster's classic book *Celebration of Discipline* reserves a whole chapter for service, saying:

> Nothing *disciplines* the inordinate desires of the flesh like service, and nothing *transforms* the desires of the flesh like serving in hiddenness. The flesh whines against service but screams against hidden service. It strains and pulls for honor and recognition. It will devise subtle, religiously acceptable means to call attention to the service rendered. If we stoutly refuse to give in to this lust of the flesh, we crucify it. Every time we crucify the flesh, we crucify our pride and arrogance.[7]

There is an older woman in my church who radiates the joy of giving. She has never been called up on stage or featured in a promo video. Yet she spends hours upon hours quietly volunteering her time and energy in one corner or another. On a cold day I find her cheerfully ready to sweep the door open as parents race their children through face-freezing wind. Late at night I find her hiding in a forgotten cubicle, balancing spreadsheets. And at midday she can be found volunteering at the front desk of our social-services program.

We know her real name, but my husband and I refer to her as "the salt of the earth." When I picture someone hearing the words "Well done, good and faithful servant," she is the one who springs to mind. Without any thought of fame or platform, she simply gives of herself joyfully.

Yet I can't follow her example—not exactly. We moms have precious few hours to clock in on church service days or the energy to volunteer after our work and home tasks are done. This discipline of service is put on hold for the time being, we say, because there are so many diapers to change, groceries to buy, and math worksheets to correct.

Oh, the irony! Not only do our days overflow with service, but our efforts are so unseen and unappreciated that *we ourselves do not realize what they are*—or that they qualify as spiritual disciplines. After all, this is simply the work that needs doing. Nothing special to see here.

I do strain and scream, as Foster predicts, when one child after the next succumbs to influenza, forcing me to rearrange my work schedule for weeks on end. I do turn toward bitterness when my energy is redirected to the discipline of service at all hours of the day and night. There is no thank-you or promotion to cheer and reward me, no chance that someone will walk around the corner and realize how quietly and joyfully I give of my time, how successfully I crucify my pride. Mothers practice daily the discipline of hidden service—so hidden we do not see it ourselves.

There is so much work to do, so much debilitating exhaustion, and the weight of it all can crush a woman who feels unsupported and invisible. We easily lose ourselves in the whirlwind, and not in a good way. The more our children require of us, the more alone we often feel. Our hours of caregiving—in the nursery, in the hallway, in the night—can be a time of lonely solitude.

But there is an opportunity buried here, a gem deeply concealed in hard rock. Will you dig with me? Can we begin to chip away at the lifeless stone to find the treasure deep inside? Staring down these disciplines in the face, and refusing the shortcuts of bitterness, we may find within our spirits fruit lying dormant. And it may burst into a flower yet.

Filthy Feet

The roads are dusty and dirty. Donkeys and horses, pigs and sheep, and shepherds and fishermen have walked these roads—and left their mark. So have the twelve men arriving to dinner, the ceremonial Passover meal. They enter the dining room to a table set low and surrounded by cushions to soften their seat on the floor. With a setup like this, feet and food are in uncomfortable relationship. The savory scents of lamb and herbs mingle with the sweaty smells of sandals.

This will never do. And so a slave or servant will be called for, to crouch down undignified on the ground and wash the waste and filth from the feet of those at dinner. So repulsive is this task that, legally, even a slave can refuse it.[8]

Perhaps that's what happened today. Perhaps these twelve friends were just too filthy for the servants to handle. Or maybe the servant girl was pregnant, unable either to crouch on the floor or to stand the smell of it. I certainly wouldn't blame her.

In any case, no lowly foot washer arrives, and instead the unthinkable happens: Jesus, the teacher, the Lord and Master, rises from his cushion and brings the basin and towel. Stooping before Peter, he begins a task too humble and undignified even for unwilling slaves.

Peter is rightly aghast. Stepping away from Jesus' towel-clad hand, he renounces even the idea of his Lord washing his putrid feet.

But Jesus continues to wash and pronounces a new reality of the Kingdom: Anyone who would associate with Jesus must accept this service. And then, having been served in such a humbling way, they are to go out and do the same to others.

Maybe Jesus' foot washing shouldn't have been so shocking, in hindsight. There was foreshadowing, certainly. Jesus crouching in the road, mixing dirt into mud with his own saliva, and giving sight to a presumed-guilty blind man. Jesus placing his hands on lepers, changing his plans to accommodate the sick and worried. He started the day with a lineup of needs that stretched never-ending: touching the sick, welcoming children, casting out demons, catching fish, feeding folks who forgot to bring their own lunch.

Just as I sneak away from my children, hoping to find a hidden corner and five minutes' peace, Jesus made his own escapes to quiet places. Just as my kids sniff out my hiding place, so Jesus' followers tracked him down too. He knew the irritation of being awoken from sleep to meet yet another need, ease another anxiety, calm another storm.

Jesus, Son of God and Word made flesh, taught us, showed us with his own two hands, aching back, and cracking knees. If meeting an onslaught of his children's physical needs day after day wasn't a waste of time for the Lord during the height of his short earthly ministry, mustn't he value our own exhausting days serving the children he gave us? If God came to earth in the position of a servant, must he not deeply value service?

Mothers serve their families in all manner of dirty and undignified positions, willingly taking on a workload so extensive and ongoing you could never hire someone to do it. To meet the unquenchable thirst of our children's needs, we empty ourselves again and again.

"I have nothing left." We have all said this at one time or another, even if no one was around to hear it. The services we perform as mothers bring us to the end of ourselves, often without support. Nothing left to feed ourselves, nothing left to give to God. No one around to pick us up off the floor.

And yet it is here, at this broken, depleted moment, that motherhood is most powerfully a spiritual practice. The goal of spiritual disciplines is to bring us to *this place*, to the place where we have lost everything but God. In this deep emptiness we must cast ourselves upon him and wait on him, for we have nothing else, no other hope.

In motherhood we are not furthest from the practices of

faith as it seems, but at the center. In this spiritual desert we touch the very pinnacle of spiritual practice.

Fertile Streams in the Desert

In Western society, parenting takes place behind closed doors, shut gates, locked vans. We can be very, very alone on these long days. Our own mothers, sisters, and friends are only a text message or Facebook status away, but we need physical touch, someone to play with the kids while we grab a shower, helpful hands bearing casserole dishes. Gone are the days of women singing call-and-response songs as they walked together to the river each morning and evening, hauling water and washing clothes together, a village of peers and mentors. These days we serve in solitude, each with our own space.

But for many moms, this is not the kind of solitude or space we need. This separateness is not a rejuvenating break to calm the weary heart. There is noise and crowding aplenty, the sounds of demanding children and even more demanding social expectations. In motherhood we can enter a solitude that is lonely and soul sapping, not reviving. Without warning, the joyful blessing of children can initiate a dark night of the soul.

To our children we embody bounty, fertility, a life-giving stream. But we ourselves are often parched, the fertile streams of our bodies flowing through the dry deserts of our souls. There may be bounty in our wombs and breasts, in our homes and car-seat-packed vans—but there is a wilderness in our spirits.

Solitude, like service, is an ancient spiritual discipline, long understood as powerfully formative. As I was painfully reminded by the conference speaker I mentioned in chapter one, people of faith are taught to find pockets of solitude on a regular basis: a thirty-minute quiet time each day at the very least. But for mothers and caregivers of all sorts, our non-negotiable acts of service can render the option of *choosing* solitude impossible. We don't have an hour a day (or even a week!) to indulge in anything at all.

But isolation—that heavy sense of being unseen and alone? That we have in plenty.

————————

She is running away or at least doing what passes for running during third-trimester pregnancy. A slave, used and abused (sexually and otherwise) by her masters, she no longer fits into their plan. Discarded. She has been impregnated by another woman's husband, on the whim of a fearful, childless wife, and her shameful reward was jealous mistreatment by the very woman who hatched this plan in the first place.

Broken and alone, pregnant with her first child, Hagar escapes into the desert. There is much more than simple geographical significance here, for the desolation is a powerful metaphor for the danger and isolation that entraps her. Yet it is in this place, in the barren wilderness, that she discovers a spring of fresh water flowing from the ground, a source of life and hope, a place of rejuvenation in the wasteland. And it is here, where water flows in the desert, that she meets the angel of the Lord.

When she leaves this powerful encounter, she declares of God, "You are the God who sees me" (Genesis 16:13).

We easily gloss over Hagar's life, reading her narrative as merely a device to move along the more important plot. In fact, this is exactly the way Abram and Sarai themselves saw her at the time. But she was a living, breathing woman with human needs and experiences. In her story we hear the cry of an isolated, abandoned mother who is seen by God. A woman driven into a desolation of solitude who nevertheless finds there the powerful, life-giving presence of the God Who Sees.

Hagar needed justice and tangible provision—there is no doubt about it. Simply singing "God Is All I Need" with a forced smile would not fill her cup; nor will it fill ours. But in the wilderness she encountered the Lord—she *saw* the One who sees her—and her strength to continue was renewed.

Mamas, we so often feel alone and unseen. We pour ourselves out day and night, and the weight of it can be so isolating. Our identity as "Mom," the source of all life for so many, can become desolation for ourselves. This is a valid, physical, human need, an emptiness that must be filled by real, physical, human companions. But in the wee hours of darkness, in our solitude, in our isolating service, he is there. He is keeping vigil with you, over you.

Our God is the one who sees you.

He will lead you beside quiet waters.

He will restore your soul.

———

Several hours into my no-longer-interrupted eight hours of nightly sleep, my fuzzy awareness is called upon to notice that something is different. A smallish creature has appeared, wormed his way between his daddy and me, and fallen asleep with one arm flung across my body. Now deeply sleeping, his body marks the time with each breath, his tummy gently pushing against my back.

Thus snuggled, the three of us keep on sleeping.

But the God Who Sees Us remains on vigil. The one who came to serve us, who got his hands dirty cooking fish for breakfast, is holding me steadfast. And in the morning his mercies will be new to comfort us. His strength will be sufficient for all the tasks that await.

SERVICE AND SOLITUDE IN PRACTICE

——— *Silence* ———

Moms don't get many silent moments. We're unlikely to even sleep or use the toilet without someone asking where we put their dinosaurs and ponies.

But we get an occasional minute here and there. We're standing in line at the library or waiting for the gas tank to fill. Every now and then we may even have a morning to ourselves! How can we use these rare miracles to feed our souls?

I don't know about you, but I tend to fill these snippets of time by scrolling through Facebook on my phone. There's nothing wrong with that—sometimes we need to just unplug and relax. Catching up with friends and current events on social media can remind us that we're intelligent, social humans, involved in a community larger than the kitchen.

But at the same time, eagerness to fill any silence with noise and information can be detrimental to our spirits. We need pockets of empty time to simply be present with ourselves—our thoughts and feelings—as well as learn to be comfortable staying present with the moment and day we're in. God's presence is available to us every second of the day, no matter how busy that second may be. By using the quieter minutes to focus our eyes on him, it becomes easier to remember him while we move through the busy times.

PRACTICE

- *Allow and embrace silence.* When you notice a sliver of quiet time, accept it mindfully. Allow it to remain silent. Resist the urge to fill it with noise of any kind—audio noise or busy noise.
- *Recenter.* Use your body—breathing, posture, facial

expression—to remind your heart and soul of God's presence. Become aware of unhelpful thought patterns (for example, *I can't believe this line is sooo slow!*). Avoid distractions that may provide entertainment but hinder rest and peace. Redirect your mind to prayer, worship, or simply resting silently in him.

• *Fill this space with grace.* Have grace for yourself; the goal is not perfection. If you can use one silent minute per day to nourish your soul, this is a win! Spend no time at all being frustrated by how long it has been since you last recentered, or discouraged by how hard it is to let go of worries (or your phone!). Just allow this moment, with yourself and God, to be what it is. And give thanks.

You keep [her] in perfect peace
 whose mind is stayed on you,
 because [she] trusts in you.
ISAIAH 26:3, ESV

———————— *Diapers* ————————

My pastor began, "Don't try to change the whole world, instead . . ." I didn't hear what he intended because the person sitting next to my toddler and me leaned over and finished the sentence: ". . . change a diaper."

This made me laugh, but it struck me as absolutely true. It feels "spiritual" to sacrifice something for strangers but less valuable when the person in need is our responsibility. But isn't part of the spiritual goal of *service* to see *all creation* as part of our shared responsibility?

Our rambunctious offspring are helpless to care for even their most basic needs, so in caring for them, we touch "the least of these" . . . and therefore Jesus himself. Changing diapers is a humbling task, both for the changer and the change-ee. Parents of infants and toddlers complete this task countless times per day, often while on the run or between other tasks. Can we touch and serve Jesus as we lift, fold, and wipe?

PRACTICE

- *Remember.* Whether you enjoy diaper changes or dread them, this is an intimate experience for both you and your baby. Focus your mind on the task, and be present with him or her, making eye and skin contact. Rejoice in the beauty of God's (and your!) creation.
- *Reflect.* Consider how vulnerable we all are to our fellow humans and how dependent we are on one another. Allow this act of humble service to nurture your sense of compassion.
- *Follow.* Jesus insisted on washing his friends' filthy feet—an appallingly dirty job in his culture. He said that when we touch someone in need, we are touching him. Remember that in changing this diaper, you are following in the footsteps of Jesus—and serving him.

The King will reply, "Truly I tell you, whatever you did for one of the least of these brothers and sisters of mine, you did for me."

MATTHEW 25:40

Work

All moms work hard—there's no doubt about that. Some of us work primarily at home, while others of us spend hours at a job or work site. Increasingly, we moms find our lives arranged with a nontraditional mix of both. If your week includes hours spent working outside the home, motherhood can be a spiritual practice while on the job.

Just as there are countless reasons why a mother might choose (or need) to stay home, there are a million reasons why a mother might choose (or need) to have a job. Going to work may not feel like a spiritual discipline, but for those who hold that responsibility, faithfully providing for the family is an act of service like any other. It is entirely possible to love and serve someone without being physically present.

PRACTICE

- *Remember.* Most of the ideas we've considered can be practiced at work—if we remember to bring them with us. Use your breathing to quiet yourself. As you walk from the car to your work space, feel the ground beneath your feet. Use the tools begun at home to remember God's presence in your work environment.

- *Reflect.* Consider all that you provide for your family through your efforts and service. Managing finances, modeling how to navigate adult scenarios and problems, and child-to-caregiver bonding are just a few. Remember that even though you are not physically with your children, your efforts are directly contributing to their care and well-being. Pray for them while you are away.
- *Gratitude.* Being employed and able to make ends meet is a tremendous blessing, even if it doesn't feel like it in the midst of the daily grind. As you arrive at work, offer the day to the Lord with thanks. Consider placing a card or picture in your work space to remind you of gratitude.

Whatever you do, work at it with all your heart, as working for the Lord, not for human masters. . . . It is the Lord Christ you are serving.

COLOSSIANS 3:23-24

CHAPTER 7

SACRIFICE AND SURRENDER

Feasting with Open Hands

IT's 3:00 P.M. ON THANKSGIVING DAY. The dried leaves and mini gourds adorning every nook and cranny perfectly complement the meandering smells of roasted turkey. Picked-over hors d'oeuvres and mugs of cider litter the living room as folks abandon the football game to gather at the table. Feast and family are gathered and ready.

You know that hungry-yet-happy feeling when the table is laid and all your loved ones circle around it? Well . . . I'm not feeling it. I'm not even at the table. A teething, nap-deprived toddler and I are squaring off in the next room. Grandma and Daddy are more than willing to take my place, but incessant "morning" sickness leaves me more likely to puke than feast. Even from two walls away, the nostalgic smells overpower my queasy tummy.

As the sounds of feasting family waft through the walls, I float away on a wave of bitterness. *Remind me what "relaxed" feels like again. How is it that the same people who get to sleep through the night are also the people who get leisure time during the day? Isn't "daily" often enough to deprive me of peaceful mealtimes? Must I give up grown-up conversation on holidays as well as All. Other. Days?*

I try to remind myself of the truth, but I'm so tired. So depleted. So immersed in this season of caregiving that I cannot see a light at the end of the tunnel—or if this *is* a tunnel. Maybe life is just like this now. Maybe eternity will be spent forever wiping other people's bodily fluids, without days off, and never getting half a night's sleep.

I recite the facts to myself, hoping one or two of them will sink in eventually: Everyone takes a turn being left out sometimes. So many suffer on holidays because of lost family, while my situation stems from abundance of family. Some are too sick to eat because of cancer or other terrifying illnesses; my nausea comes from the miracle of new life. Others work endlessly to avoid starvation, whereas I am comfortably raising small children.

I've spent half a lifetime present at the feasting table, with half a lifetime of Thanksgivings on the way. Just this one year (well, okay, maybe off and on for a decade) of sick kids, fussy toddlers, and pregnancy symptoms—just this small sacrifice—and what an amazing payoff! The chance to make a person, to mother my children—an opportunity many would give anything to have.

Or so I tell myself while I bounce my drooling toddler. Pop quiz, hot shot. Which of these statements is true?

A. My difficulties are literally Thanksgiving burdens. They spring from bounty and abundance and point to blessing in every respect.
B. My difficulties require difficult, costly sacrifices.
C. I have a choice to make. I can fight with bitterness against these sacrifices, or I can surrender to them.

The answer is D: All of the above.

There are many forces that form our spirits, and two of the most potent are sacrifice and surrender. How we respond to them will determine if we emerge from life strong and beautiful or brittle and bitter.

And in motherhood, we meet these twin crucibles every single day.

Pee on the Floor and Other Problems

"I have no control over how much pee is on my floor," my friend texts me, home with a quiverful of preschoolers. Another friend, a mom of tweens, confides the truth to me over coffee: The children she gave birth to are their own selves. She cannot control their emotions, responses, thoughts, or spiritual choices.

Meanwhile, one of my best friends is in the hospital

recovering from an emergency C-section, her premature infant in the NICU. Another is fretting over a teenager hospitalized last week with unexplainable health problems. Still another just sent her closest friends a devastating email: After years of infertility, their almost-completed adoption process fell through.

From start to finish, motherhood is an exercise in sacrifice and surrender.

Sacrifice and surrender are with us at the very beginning, even before motherhood, before conception. Some of us launch into maternity with devastating news—an unexpected pregnancy, too young, with a man on his way out, after rape or abuse, or with a frightening diagnosis. The other side of the coin is equally devastating—the slammed doors of hope, the shattering news of infertility, miscarriage, pain, loss, death.

These days we marry when we choose to. We marry for love and have an arsenal of birth control and family-planning resources on hand. Yet our beloved ideal of "choice" is mostly a mirage, for whether we become mothers, and when exactly, is still outside our control. Family making is an all-or-nothing game, with no rigging the system. Monthly blood begins to flow, or it doesn't. The adoption falls through, or we receive a midnight call that a baby needs a home *tonight, right now.* However we arrive at motherhood, we must surrender to it, with no warning.

Once pregnancy is underway, sacrifice and surrender are thick as thieves. A *child* is developing in our wombs! There's no way to take a breather (or in the third trimester, a breath). And yet in the midst of the sacrifice comes the surrender.

Pregnancy is an amazing paradox. From the unknowns of conception to the waiting at the end, and through the harrowing hours of labor and delivery, we mothers play the most crucial, self-sacrificing role—and yet a passive role. My body toils, bearing the full brunt of the strain, yet my brain and will are not allowed to call the shots or make the plans.

We are like women possessed. While these children could not be conceived, developed, cared for, or birthed without our bodies pouring themselves out in every possible way, without pause, twenty-four hours a day—in the most bizarre way everything happens *to* us. We have been overtaken. Our hopes and plans play a very little role in the whole business. When else are we so completely consumed, required of, demanded of, and taken from—yet so not under our own power?

In pregnancy we have no choice but to surrender to this life force. It demands everything of us, and for many women it demands even their life. We cannot decline or alter the road ahead, no matter how grim it becomes. These things are required of us, *exacted from* us.

Meanwhile there are no guarantees that a healthy baby will make it to a safe, full-term birth. Whether you have a normal or high-risk pregnancy, there are no promises. Pregnant mothers undergo a daily practice of surrender.

Labor is the exclamation point to this bizarre paradox. It's a breathtaking fact that I have no idea how to birth a baby—but my body does. I do not know how to heal afterward or make milk inside my breasts—but my body does. I didn't know how to make this baby in the first place, yet my body did it anyway. And my body *will* do all of these things when the ball is set in motion. With or without my consent.

Just like conception, birth may come too soon and too suddenly: a rushed trip to the ER or a newborn delivered in the subway. For others, endless waiting is required—waiting, waiting for the unknown hour we cannot begin to predict or choose. Either way, the birthing pains begin. There is no escaping the realities and work that lie ahead. In these harrowing hours we offer up our body and breath for the life of a child. We surrender to sacrifice, to pain, to the possibility of life or death in order to usher new life into the world.

And then the baby! Ultrasounds tell us far more than we used to know ahead of time. Yet this little bundle is a complete mystery, hidden away in the secret place. What will he look like? Will she be healthy? Special needs? Difficult or charming personality? Entirely in the dark, we mamas commit ourselves forever, body and soul. I will embrace this unknown person into myself, into my family, into my future, not just for the unknowns of today but for the unknowns of forever. Everything this child is and will be I welcome in the midst of all that is most sacred to me, heedlessly, without restraint. No holds barred.

Birth comes like victory. We summited peaks thought unscalable, and we have won. Yet motherhood is just beginning. This new infant requires constant attention and doesn't even smile in return. Broken and torn from delivery, exhausted from pregnancy, we now rise to the challenge of providing twenty-four-hour care to a vulnerable infant. New mamas wade through sleep deprivation and screaming nipples without one hour a day to attend to their own basic needs. These first months of motherhood present a crash course in surrender and sacrifice.

As months and years pass, it gets easier. Two hours of sleep work back up to seven or eight. But motherhood gets harder, too. The children clinging tightly to us suddenly hit the ground running and move ever further and farther away.

It is terrifying to look at your heart, your very best self, walking around outside your body, as they say. Willing and able to walk away, willing and able to make or break the life you so painstakingly created. This is how it should be, of course. Our babies, grown and strong, their lives the costly, precious gift we gave to them and did not, could not, would not take back.

Once again our companions are sacrifice and surrender, for we can feed, clothe, teach, discipline, and nurture, but we do not make our children, and we do not control them. Each one is a unique creation, a mysterious combination of genetics and experience—growing up.

We pour ourselves out to let go.

There are no guarantees in this task, mama. Not ever. The same pangs of worry we feel during the early cramping and spotting of first-trimester pregnancy can make themselves at home for the rest of our lives, if we let them. Just as our bodies are overtaken by a growing child, our spirits can be overtaken with anxiety. We will expand to accommodate our fears, however large they grow.

These babies did not exist just years ago or even moments ago, but now we cannot survive without them. There are no guarantees. Not even a hint of certainty. Despite countless attempts, God continues to refuse my negotiations. All the contracts I've sent up to the Creator have been returned unsigned.

And so the outcome of all our love, sacrifice, and surrender is itself a complete secret. Accepting this, too, is its own surrender.

Rip Currents

We are scampering along the sandy beach on an almost-warm day, exploring tide pools, running in and out of the waves. Between discoveries, my husband, once an ocean lifeguard, instructs our novice swimmers about rip currents.

Rip currents form when the water washed to shore by waves heads back out to sea in a dangerously powerful rush. If you're caught in one, trying to swim home to shore is like running from a fire on a treadmill—you'll exhaust yourself without making progress. Tragically, the very act of saving yourself will destroy you.

The secret is to fight the panic and simply relax. Float for a while, and the current will eventually lose momentum;

then swim parallel to the shore to escape the current's width, and you can float back to shore on the waves.

The life-or-death challenge is determining when fighting for your life means letting go and giving in to the current.

Occasionally when I close my eyes to pray, I see myself in a similar situation. I'm fighting for my life, trying desperately to swim out of troubled waters. It's clear that the water represents the chaos of my life—my fears, the future, things I can neither control nor survive.

The flowing water crushes, and I cannot heave myself out. The force has nearly overwhelmed me. I'm about to go under.

At this point I have two choices. Continue to fight (as my instinct demands), but not succeed. Or . . . let go. The second choice requires so much courage to release my fears and my need for control and certainty. But if I submit my tired body to the stubborn waves, my struggle will be replaced with rest.

Ironically, the fight to save myself is what will actually destroy me. When I open my tired hands and surrender, I am at rest. The current pulls me swiftly but peacefully now that I lie still. The flowing water is no longer dangerous but life-giving. With my struggling over, I see the beauty that was always here, the incredible transcendence all around me.

We're still in the water, my sister. We are not safely on a blanket at the shore, sipping lemonade. But in the midst of our chaos and sacrifice there can be peace and release. Here in the midst of our crazy life we may yet taste the beauty and glory of God's presence.

Of course, all this talk of water and waves is only metaphor. But doesn't it tell the truth of sacrifice and surrender? The horrors of our past and the nightmares of our future hold us in bondage, as though paying a ransom in the currency of worry might somehow set us free. We kick and scream against those things we hate and fear but cannot change—but God invites us to let go and find his presence in this moment.

We can fight, but death will sweep us away. Or we can stop this scuffle for control and fall, fumbling and awkward, into life.

Ignoring this invitation to surrender is so very tempting. In the face of sacrifice we want to grasp—to plan, negotiate, and demand. With each dream and freedom that we lose, bitterness becomes more tempting. It is for this very reason that spiritual journeys have always included surrender. The disciplines invite us to sprinkle our days with prayer, meditation, fasting, worship, silence, simple living, and other practices that teach our spirits to release into *his* Spirit. Each discipline is meant to tear our eyes and fierce grip off of ourselves and place them on him. They coax us to let go of all we cling to and accept something better from his hands.

Our surrender to God does not mean bondage. Rather, surrender is the path *out* of bondage. With his help we release our grip on the things that shackle us. When we are at his feet, he consumes us, burning away our self-centeredness, fear, anxiety, pride, judgments, insecurities—and filling us instead with himself.

Sacrifice and surrender are our offering to God, but they are also his gift to us.

The trick is knowing what sort of current has captured us. Is this the time to fight or the time to let go? With that old, famous prayer we plead, "God, give us grace to accept with serenity the things that cannot be changed, courage to change the things that should be changed, and the wisdom to distinguish the one from the other."[9]

On the day I found out I was going to be a mother for the first time, I felt my heart pound in dread as the doctor declared my pregnancy high risk, with a likelihood of early miscarriage. My pregnancy-test emotions, swinging between shock and excitement, took a hard detour toward debilitating panic.

As I stood in my living room, I realized what choosing a life of love-induced anxiety would entail. It meant that, should I make it through the first trimester, there were two more trimesters to worry through. It meant that anything and everything could go wrong during labor and delivery. It meant that infants were so vulnerable, and SIDS was never out of the question. It meant my growing child would teeter toward swimming pools and busy highways, dangerous addictions and extreme sports. Starting this journey with worry, I knew I would *never* find a finish line. Prenatal worry, even when warranted, was the beginning of a life sentence.

And so, with one hand outstretched to God and the other embracing my belly and the too-tiny-to-see cells that are now my ten-year-old son, I made a decision: surrender. That day, in that moment, I was a mother. There was life inside me that, with the help of God, I had created. Whatever might come, in this moment I would rejoice, I would be present, I would open my heart to all the dangers and joys of love and life for as long as I had them.

In motherhood, we meet the twin spiritual disciplines of sacrifice and surrender up close and so very personally. But take heart, mama. Surrender is not a promise that our hands will always be open—it simply means granting God eternal permission to pry open our clenched fists.

SACRIFICE AND SURRENDER IN PRACTICE

Pain

Motherhood, with all its joy and beauty, has a close relationship with pain. It begins, of course, with the aches and dangers of pregnancy, then labor and delivery. Maternity has threatened—and taken—women's lives since the beginning.

Before any chance of recovery comes the pain of

sleeplessness, the strain of changing relationships and identity, the weight of isolation, the agony of loss. Some mothers experience the unthinkable pain of losing a child. Many mothers experience some form of postpartum depression.[3] And for all of us, we go through the mixed and complicated emotions of raising children—then letting them go, sometimes facing rejection or judgment from the ones we gave our lives to birth and raise.

Pain and suffering have always been the midwives of spiritual maturity. People who suffer and survive have a depth of wisdom that is hard-earned and validated. Some religious traditions take this too far, directing spiritual seekers to artificially empty their lives of pleasure and fill them instead with pain. But our goal is to find God in our present reality—both the pleasure *and* the pain. They are, after all, the twin sides of our human experience.

Both in deep seasons of tragedy or depression, and in our day-to-day pain and trials, we have an opportunity to throw ourselves upon God. Suffering forces our focus on to the highest priority; we let go of the insignificant and grasp what matters most.

Without a doubt, and without any searching on our part, pain will find each one of us—each and every day. Though

---

[3] Friend, postpartum depression is *real*, terrible, and dangerous. It can strike anybody—this is a chemical situation and has nothing to do with you being a "good mom" or "good Christian." PPD can develop even months after your baby is born. If you are suffering from darkness, depression, or thoughts of harming yourself or others, please seek professional help. You might begin with your ob-gyn, your personal doctor, or whoever delivered your baby. Any of these professionals should be trained in spotting, and treating, PPD. There is help for you, sister, and *you are worth helping*.

pain is not here for us to embrace, it can act as a powerful spiritual tool.

PRACTICE

- *Be honest.* Whether you're suffering from plugged nursing ducts or postpartum depression, the loneliness of an emptying nest or a child's destructive choices, there is no benefit in pretending pain isn't there when it is. Be honest with yourself about what is happening and how you feel about it. Be honest with trusted friends—even if this requires great courage. Seek compassionate, professional help when you need it. Anguish is terrible. When we deny that we're suffering, we let the pain control and destroy us. In naming our pain, we have the chance to survive and even grow in the process.

- *Seek God.* Just as the hunger pains of fasting remind us to let go of self-reliance and throw ourselves on God, the ache of life reminds us to seek him. There are many ways to do this, so find one that fits your temperament and situation. Sing a worship song, proclaiming a beauty that flies in the face of despair. Pray over and over "Jesus Christ, Son of God, have mercy on me" as you go through your day. Light a candle to remember that there is a flicker of light the darkness has not overcome. Kneel on the ground and practice surrendering to him, waiting for his fullness. Physically, literally hold up your hands to him, through tears if need be, just as your children do when they need your comfort.

- *Keep walking.* Some days we have to keep putting one foot in front of the other, even when we see no light ahead. Sometimes we have to just walk until one day we realize we're in a better place than where we started. Treat the pain of life as you did the contractions of labor: Can I do this forever? No. But can I do it for ten minutes? Yes. And then ten more. And then ten more.

We know that suffering produces perseverance; perseverance, character; and character, hope.

ROMANS 5:3-4

Driving

We've all been there—stuck in a car with crying children, or a baby who won't sleep, or a toddler who just fell asleep but should have been awake. Maybe we're driving alone but traffic is horrible, or we're stuck waiting for the second train in a row to pass and we're already late getting home. Driving anywhere can be stressful, especially when we have a car full of hungry kids, or we're running late for soccer or music class, or we're hurrying home from work in rush-hour traffic.

So what better place to embrace an organic, homegrown spiritual discipline? This is where we are, this moment. We're not setting aside time we don't have—instead, an opportunity for spiritual practice unfolds right inside our routine. Here in close quarters with demanding people, we have a chance to cultivate patience that could never be duplicated in a prayer chapel.

Any novice can be patient and mindful of God's presence while sitting in peaceful silence. But achieving a cheerful, long-suffering attitude in the car is doctoral-level spiritual formation—if not superhuman.

PRACTICE

- *Remember.* The biggest battle we face in stressful daily situations is remembering what we want. We get caught up in the noise and the crowd and the schedule, and any thought of staying present with God's Spirit rushes out the window. Consider placing a card or a symbol—like a cross or Bible verse—in the car where you'll see it (without obstructing your vision). Use this to set your mind back on the goal.
- *Open to perspective.* Once you become aware of yourself, find small steps to center your thoughts. Take deep breaths. Open your hands (if you're stopped!) and let go with acceptance: The train will not move faster if our bodies are tense and clenched and our tone harsh and angry.
- *Watch your words.* A crowded car can bring out the worst in everyone, and our own frustrations may be compounded by fighting, whining children. As you begin to recenter yourself, try to practice patience

aloud. Instead of saying, "I can't believe you made us late to church again," try, "Well, we're going to be late—but look at that beautiful autumn tree! I'm so glad we got to see that together." It may sound fake at first; it may even *be* fake at first! This is practice. As you go, the change will seep through your words into your heart and take root.

> *In their hearts humans plan their course,*
> *but the LORD establishes their steps.*
>
> PROVERBS 16:9

Clutter

I can't stand clutter. And yet, any and every empty surface in my house seems to attract *stuff* like a magnet, becoming a shrine to chaos, a symbol of the never-ending chore lists that surround my days. As they say, trying to clean a house with children in it is like brushing your teeth while eating Oreo cookies. Beautifully staged catalog homes are for some other season of life, and I've made my peace with that. But the clutter wears on me even so.

Piles of laundry, toys, and school papers don't make for the same prayerful ambience as a quiet, candlelit room. Yet mindfully clearing a room or a table of clutter can be a practical and powerfully calming exercise. What if freshening a room could refresh our spirits as well?

Find one area of your home to declutter. Start small; the goal here is not a house clean from top to bottom. Choose the kitchen table, or the mantel, or a small room. Then, slowly and intentionally, pick up each thing that needs clearing, one at a time. As you set one small area of your world back to harmony, breathe deeply and allow your mind and emotions to declutter as well. Allow this chore to cleanse your spirit in addition to your home.

Within minutes, more bills, dust, and crumbs will find their way to settle on this clean space, but that is okay too. You might want to choose one surface to keep clear, representing the peace in your spirit—or you may just let it go and rejoice in the chaos of life until you're ready to practice decluttering again.

PRACTICE

- *Start small.* Choose just one place in your house to start with. As you continue in the practice over time, perhaps one day you will mindfully clean your entire house and spirit. For now, begin with one table or room.
- *Work mindfully.* Rushing will result in a quickly cleaned area, but our goal is primarily spiritual. How can you use this necessary chore to feed your soul? Remove the clutter and dirt slowly enough to feel the impact on decluttering your spirit as well.
- *Give thanks.* As you pick up the socks and empty cups, remember the people who left them there and

the blessing they add to your life. Offer up a prayer of blessing for them. Once the desk or coffee table is clear, enjoy it. Light a candle in the center, or run your hand across the clean upholstery. Thank God for his work in making things new.

Do not remember the former things,
*   or consider the things of old.*
I am about to do a new thing;
*   now it springs forth, do you not perceive it?*
I will make a way in the wilderness
*   and rivers in the desert.*

ISAIAH 43:18-19, NRSV

CHAPTER 8

PERSEVERANCE

Sweet Grapes

"IT'S GONNA TAKE one hundred and forty-four years," she moans dramatically, tragically. My preschool daughter has been sitting, focused, tugging at a new pair of socks. She's determined to get them on correctly and needs my help. But there's a major hiccup: I'm in the shower, covered in suds. And waiting is not a three-year-old's cup of tea.

"One hundred and forty-four!" she echoes, yelling, kicking her still-bare feet against the wall. Then she gasps and screams as though in terror. "Mommy! You have to come *now*! My bottom hurts from sitting too long!"

Apparently her bottom recovers, because later in the day she is sitting again. This time she's on the time-out step, scowling, arms crossed. This is one formidable young lady. "Time out is *over*," she shouts.

"Not until you're ready to clean up this mess you made," I remind her.

"*That's not going to EVER BE UNTIL ALL DAY!!!*" she declares to the universe.

She's probably right. I'm not sure if I should laugh or cry. These days it's all about the marathon. There's no sprinting in motherhood, no *hurry up* or *get it done*. We are coaxing and waiting, training and enticing. Each moment drifts down and piles up around us. We might sit all day waiting for a precious someone to eat his peas or clean up toys or find the courage to mutter, "I'm sorry." Since the shoes must all be tied "myself!" we may never leave the house again. We attack our own chores just as stubbornly, staring at a bleak unbalanced budget as long as it takes to find enough money for a seven-year-old's beloved karate class.

Mothers persevere. We find a way to make it happen, to provide for our children and get it all done. We dig deep and sign on for the long haul.

We keep going.

———————

With all its joys, trials, and demands, motherhood is packed full of spiritual practices. Undergirding them all is the discipline of perseverance.

It looks different in every stage and season. Throughout pregnancy, we persevere through sickness, back pain, and upheaval of all kinds. Labor and delivery offers only one way to escape with our lives: Continue forward.

Perseverance wears a different face for mothers walking through infertility or grief, for the family waiting on adoption papers or the judge's ruling on foster placement. The first-time mom faces a different shade of perseverance than the mother of five kids under age seven. Through financial troubles and marriage problems, perseverance tags along like a shadow. Single moms persevere. Young moms and older moms, mamas with babies, teenagers, and grown kids. Perseverance changes color and shape and size, but she is always, always at our backs, pushing us forward.

Through sleeplessness and sickness, sacrifice and service, we dig deep and keep going. Whatever else may be required of us, this engine propels us day after day, through all our care and nurture, in each day spent at home or at work, in every aspect of our identity. We are making lunches and unbuckling car seats and sorting through footie sleepers— and we are persevering. No matter what difficulties flood our minds and hearts, we put one step in front of the next, tackling the next task, getting up again today and tomorrow and the day after that. Everything we have walked through in all of these pages was made possible by perseverance.

Moms keep going.

With the Morning

I wake up and immediately know something is different. The wind has changed, the sun is shining, and the snow drip, drip, drips off my eaves as it melts. We've survived so very many months of cold shadows. The darkness bewitched us, convinced us new life was never coming. But then, without warning, resurrection is here. Before I even saw a bend in the road we turned the corner. All of sudden, creation is on the other side of death.

My family and I throw open the windows, paw through boxes for T-shirts, walk out the door, and just *breathe*. Letting the sun warm our skin, we gulp down the gift of fresh air and hope of new life. We cannot possibly get enough.

The joys of spring ebb and flow with each day, of course. A freezing, cloudy morning follows the sunny one; snow falls and buries the bikes my boys left in the yard. The transition feels like a taunt, a cruel trick. But slowly by slowly, we're getting there. Spring has reached critical mass; new life is a sure thing now.

The minute the ground thaws we're in the garden, running fingers through cool, moist soil, sorting out the spring seeds to plant: carrots, lettuce, peas. But my attention focuses on the bulbs I planted last fall. Each day I stare at the dirt, waiting for a sign. Under the ground lies the promise of tulips and daffodils, garlic and shallots and onions. If we planted them in the warmth of spring, nothing would happen at all. Strangely enough, these plants need the winter, the dormant period spent frozen in the dark underworld, to thrive.

Sure enough, it is these plants, the ones that survived their dance with darkness and near-death, that herald the good news. Brave green tips break through the still nearly frozen soil and into the sunshine, and we *know* life has made it through.

We earthbound creatures savor spring because of *perseverance*. We drink in the sun because we have been incapacitated by cold. We frolic in green grass and spring blossoms because we know the press of death and darkness.

Weeping remains for the long, cold night. The darkness can last so long we forget anything else exists. But we keep going. We persevere. And then, long after we thought to look for it, *joy* comes with the morning.

Sweet and Sour Grapes

In Western society, we value things that are easy and comfortable—*immediately* if possible. The thought of waiting more than two days for a package I ordered is unthinkable (not to mention going to the mall to hunt it down in the first place)! Speaking of hunting, we like our food nicely packaged and ready to go; no more year-round struggles with nature to keep the pantry stocked. Thanks to K-cups, ten agonizing minutes seem unreasonable to wait for coffee. My phone satisfies any and every curiosity that crosses my mind, right here and now—any piece of news, the moment it happens, anywhere in the world. And of course I stream my shows whenever I feel like it, regardless of the network's schedule.

Yes, convenience and immediacy are king, and for the most part I'm grateful; I couldn't live my modern, multifaceted life any other way.

But the determined voice of wisdom calls through the storm of swirling data. With gentle insistence, she reminds us it is not ease but *challenge* that shapes our character into strength and beauty. The ease I long for is a rascal, more than happy to lull me right into the comfort of decay.

This adorably drooling baby did not learn to crawl by sitting contentedly on his blanket, but through consternation and frustration: A toy fell out of reach and he had to stretch for it. Her muscles strengthened and her imagination lengthened, all because of desires unmet but doggedly, stubbornly pursued. If you have one of these enchanting creatures, give it a try and watch this captivating process: From the very beginning, we grow and mature because problems propel us toward solutions. Hunger drives us to attain what we do not have; discomforts push us through frustrations. So our babies grow strong, creative, and smart—because they persevere.

In the same way, our adult minds and bodies do not thrive through comfort, but challenge. Life throws a million curveballs demanding brave responses. By walking through the darkness, taking every despairing step until we reach the land of dawn—this is how we learn to love goodness, to sacrifice for beauty, and to cultivate enough hope for the next time. Even if next time the valley is darker and longer than before.

———

How did grapes become such a childhood food icon? I don't like them, and I enjoy washing and cutting them even less. But my children can't get enough if they're sweet and firm.

My kids have very selective fruit palates, and sour, wrinkly grapes wind up piled in the corner.

Here's some interesting trivia about grape cultivation: If the vines are given all the water, nutrients, and sunlight they need, they produce poor fruit. The harvest is strongest and sweetest when the vines are stressed and struggling.

Of course, the plants require enough of their basic needs met to stay alive but not enough to relax and grow complacent. The gardener has to keep the vine on its toes, so to speak, if the vineyard is to produce an abundance of sweet grapes.

I've never thought of myself as resembling a fruit cluster on a woody vine, but this is one thing we have in common; with too much ease *or* too much distress, we humans fail to thrive. We need enough to survive and sufficient discomfort to push us forward. We need an incentive to keep moving, learning, working, and striving. Only with the opportunity to practice perseverance do we produce a bountiful harvest of sweet fruits.

Eugene Peterson describes our spiritual life as a "long obedience in the same direction."[10] We can't just order up virtue when we need it or find inner strength on the DVR and Amazon Prime. To grow spiritually, we must stand squarely before a challenge and begin walking: small step after small step. Through the exciting years and the discouraging years. Through the easy times and the hard ones. Continuing faithfully in the same direction. The journey of a thousand steps can't be made in an airplane; we only arrive if we keep going through blood and sweat and tears.

Fortunately for our souls, we moms have this covered. Motherhood is such a very long obedience, and it is most certainly in the same direction.

Love Suffers Long and Is Kind

For mothers, perseverance isn't really an option. Perseverance has us in a corner and isn't willing to negotiate; continuing is the only way to stay alive. After all, labor pains can't be put on hold just because we're tired. Either we push through (literally) or we die. Colicky babies don't start cooing just because we've lost our minds from bouncing them up and down for hours. And our older children still need tough love when their choices have eroded our lives and sanity.

At the same time, perseverance isn't a given. We've all seen what happens when a mother doesn't persevere. The stakes are high for us, and there's no getting around that. We're in a do-or-die scenario.

But most of us, most of the time, keep choosing "do." Not ever perfectly. Like our diaper-clad toddlers, we plop on our bums just as often as we rise triumphantly. But through failures and mistakes, we keep going. We make these strong choices day after day after day.

1 Corinthians 13 has this to say:

Love is patient, love is kind. It does not envy, it does not boast, it is not proud. It does not dishonor others, it is not self-seeking, it is not easily angered, it keeps

no record of wrongs. Love does not delight in evil but
rejoices with the truth. It always protects, always trusts,
always hopes, always perseveres.

I CORINTHIANS 13:4-7

I love the way the New King James translates that first sentence: "Love suffers long and is kind." Could there be a better tagline for moms? *Love suffers long and is kind.* This could be our motto, printed on all our bumper stickers and T-shirts.

But my love doesn't do this, actually. My love suffers a short while and gets impatient. It suffers hardly at all and loses its cool. In addition to the T-shirt, I may need to tattoo this verse on my hand, for these six words capture enough spiritual discipline to last me a lifetime.

Hallelujah for that! We are practicing. Because we are not perfect, will never be perfect, don't *need* to be perfect, our children give us the gift of *practice*. Each and every day, motherhood provides me with all the raw materials I need to jump into an intensive course on perseverance. Every single hour I am offered the chance to try *one more time* to suffer long and be kind, to persevere.

As Eugene Peterson says,

Perseverance does not mean "perfection." It means that we keep going. We do not quit when we find that we are not yet mature and there is a long journey still before us. We get caught yelling at our wives, at our husbands, at our friends, at our employers, at our employees, at our children. Our yelling (though not all of it!) means we care about something. . . . For perseverance is not resignation.[11]

It's hard to imagine how my struggles make the harvest of my life sweeter and more abundant, like the stressed-out grapes. But we do keep going. We get up every day and keep on loving, keep on serving. After too many sleepless hours with a screaming infant, we let the baby cry safely in his crib for ten minutes so we can get a grip. We play cartoons long enough to open the window and take a deep breath in peace. We get up and work our shift even though there was no sleep the night before. We apologize for blowing it and sign up for another try.

Or to paraphrase Chumbawamba, *We get knocked down, but we get up again. You're never going to keep us down.*[12]

Amazingly, somewhere in the piles of these tiny, futile-seeming long obediences in the same direction, our children grow and keep growing. And we do too, sister. If, in the thick of sacrifice and service, life-giving and nurture, we choose life over bitterness, then these years of perseverance will take their beautiful, inevitable toll on our scarred but healing hearts.

Like a bulb that can only burst into springtime blossoms if first left underground all the cold, dead winter long, perseverance works in our souls powerfully when we feel nearly dead and long forgotten.

Somehow, in all this, we grow strong and lovely.

Wonder Women

Corrie ten Boom put aside her privilege to save lives and endured the Nazi concentration camps. Susan B. Anthony stood against oppression and fought for women's right to vote. Rosa Parks *sat* against oppression and ignited a movement of justice for African Americans. Mother Teresa gave her life to care for the dying poor. Amy Carmichael left her homeland to rescue young orphans from the sex trade and remained in her adopted country even through decades of illness. Malala Yousafzai defended her—and all female children's—right to go to school, nearly at the cost of her own life.

None of these women achieved their dreams by demanding immediate returns. Each one of them stood their ground, no matter what happened. By digging in their heels, in some cases until death, they reaped their harvest. And so we know them as heroes, as wonder women. And though we remember them for what they achieved, it was all gained through perseverance.

I know another wonder woman, another hero of perseverance. Her life is not unusual, but no less amazing for her commonality. She is approachable and remarkable but so human. Her challenges are daunting but relatable.

She is up before dawn, bouncing up and down the hallway, trying to soothe a teething baby back to sleep without waking the family. Just as she settles him, and then herself, the older children have jumped into her bed; it's morning now. She is making breakfast, packing lunches, choosing outfits, sorting shoes, signing papers.

The sun is high in the sky as she types a report with one hand, holding the breastfeeding baby with the other. She is moving on the laundry and taking something out of the freezer for dinner. She is working through wailing and tantrums, talking through conflicts and flying toys. She is leaving the office in time to get the kids—buckling them in, listening, talking, helping. She is going through the drive-through, changing out of her uniform, punching out at the time clock. She is picking up toys and watching the deathly slow minutes click by one at a time. She is sorting shoes again, signing more papers, unpacking lunches, stripping off outfits.

After dusk she tucks them all in finally, then tucks them in again. She is tired herself, but still standing, washing dishes. She is sitting down with a cup of tea and an open textbook or with a glass of wine and a laptop. She is putting a uniform on for the night shift or rocking the bouncy chair with one foot as she sorts through bills. She is opening her heart to her husband, or her mother, or her sister, or a friend. She is at home watching TV, again, with children too young to leave alone and no money for a sitter. She is collapsing into bed, trying not to notice what the clock says or calculate how many hours until the next person under her care is due to waken.

It's you, mama. You are a hero of perseverance.

Being a mother means giving as much as required to make do, to make it through. Sometimes this means working nights and weekends to pay the rent and grocery bills. Sometimes this means long hours home alone with babies and preschoolers. Sometimes this means missing sleep and meals for so long we stop feeling human. Sometimes it means battling cancer or crippling disease with fear and courage. Sometimes it means doing the work of two parents instead of one.

It means keeping on keeping on. Enduring.

It means continuing after we're tired, getting up when we're sick. It means keeping a precious daughter in time-out, even when it hurts. It means keeping a son home from his game after he cheated, even though now he won't speak to you. It means sounding out c-a-t and m-a-t again and again and reading *Green Eggs and Ham* until we can make it all the way through, with perfectly timed page turns, without ever opening an eye. It means tying shoes seven times every day, explaining again how the bunny ears go under the tunnel before they tighten. It means using the tantrums and fighting to teach life lessons. It means staying calm enough to recognize what our feelings are saying and choosing to act in a healthy way. It means taking off the training wheels and jogging with one hand on our daughter's bicycle forever.

Motherhood is perseverance.

———

After an endless night of labor, new life is born with the sunrise. After the unrelenting cold and dark of winter, spring arrives triumphantly. Our spirits have gone dormant as we put one foot in front of the other for so long we've lost track of the journey—but we awaken to find that perseverance has developed into character, and character into hope. And this hope does not disappoint us.

My son asks me to tuck him in. Such a grown-up boy he is now, sleeping so high up in the top bunk, surrounded by books instead of stuffed animals. I climb up the ladder, scrunching my head and shoulders against the sloped ceiling. As I place my head against his, he asks, "What do you want most in the world, Mom?"

My brain spins for a moment, but the answer is so easy. "You," I answer. "You and your brother and sister."

He smiles.

"I'm so lucky," I add, mostly to myself. "Because I have what I want most in the world."

Then I ask him the same question. "I want to have stronger faith," he answers, my philosopher son, who has wrestled courageously since diapers with the deepest of questions.

Oh, my son, me too. *I want that one too.* So, still hunched over the railing, feet on the ladder, back pushed against the ceiling, I tell him about the frustrated baby boy who lost his toy—and learned to crawl. About the struggling grapes that persevered and became sweet. About the tiny bulbs that waited through months of cold and burst into flower. About the muscles of our faith that are strengthened not by ease and rest but by bouncing around on doubts and questions, darkness and struggle.

Motherhood asks—demands—that we persevere for hours, days, months, years. Sometimes we see the relief, the reward, the fruit. Sometimes we release it into the universe, into God's hands, and hold ourselves open only to hope. But just as our children struggle so desperately to ride a bike, form an apology, make a new friend—and finally overcome—we are going to make it through these years, one hour, one day at a time.

We keep going.

There's no time now for silence and reflection, so we won't notice that our hearts and minds are being made new. Deep, deep roots are developing while we are too busy persevering to notice.

One day, in the quiet peace of another season, may you stumble upon a nearly forgotten garden and find it bursting forth with the resilient, lovely fruit and flowers of spring. And may it dawn on you, mama, as you walk through with wonder, that this garden is the harvest of your own brave life.

PERSEVERANCE IN PRACTICE

Routine

Our Creator formed order out of chaos. He created the cycles and seasons—never ending, always repeating—and it is by this order that we live our lives. In the busy yet monotonous days, we mothers also create routines, and in these cycles our children learn to navigate the world. As we form routines, we reflect our Creator, and as we walk through routines, we follow a path of spiritual discipline.

Cooking a meal, then cooking another. Signing school reading logs every single morning. Singing the same monotonous song every night at bedtime, twice. Driving to school for drop-off and pickup, same time, every day. Softball practice on Tuesday, piano lessons on Wednesday, Girl Scouts on Thursday. Nursing every two hours. Every two hours. Every two hours.

Doing the same things over and over again can feel oppressive. But in the numbing cycle of routine there is an opportunity to practice contentment and meditation. We reflect the cycles God created as we work among them—each morning, noon, evening, and night has its own tasks; each summer and winter has a different challenge.

We can approach these tasks as burdens—or we can approach them as spiritual tools. Prayer, worship, meditation, fasting—these traditional disciplines are intended to be done routinely: daily, weekly, annually. These practices rely on the principle of repetition to mold our spirits over time. Moms may be too pressed to add in additional habits, so why not allow our spirits to be molded by the routines we have to observe anyway? We can cultivate a growing awareness of serving God, of nurturing and creating life. We can practice the presence of God. We can learn to live meditatively.

PRACTICE

- *Be aware.* It can be tempting—or necessary!—to rush through our routine tasks. As often as possible, stay present with your schedule and your day. Feel the floor beneath your feet as you walk here and there. Notice how this part of the day leads into that one. Breathe deeply and stay "awake" during your routine cycles.

- *Give thanks.* Though certain routines may seem draining, each situation and event is a symbol of something alive. Give thanks for the children whose lives revolve around predictable meals and naps. Praise God for educational opportunities and enough time and money for extracurriculars.

- *Give love and life.* Being faithful in these routines—whether those required by an infant, a school child, or a teenager—makes up a great deal of motherhood. It is here that we persevere with care and love for our children. Place reminders by your nursing chair, dishwasher, or key chain that in these repetitive acts you create an orderly, predictable world of love and life for your children.

Do your best to present yourself to God as one approved, a worker who does not need to be ashamed.
2 TIMOTHY 2:15

Gratitude

Gratitude is a spiritual discipline that can be practiced no matter what our day holds—for whether our day is busy or quiet, hard or easy, our attitude always comes along. I tell my

kids that attitudes are a magic wand: They can take something wonderful and make it miserable or take something
miserable and make it okay.

Wisdom and spiritual teachers have always recommended
gratitude as a powerful ally. Now even science has demon-
strated the powerful effects of cultivating gratitude. A grateful lifestyle can improve your relationships, sleep, mental and
physical health, and self-esteem.

Some days we badly need a trusted shoulder to cry on.
Gratitude is not about ignoring our real pain or situations
that call for action. In fact, gratitude *never* ignores the trials;
rather, gratitude highlights the gifts and gently moves them
over to center stage, allowing us to generate the strength we
need to combat real problems.

PRACTICE

- *Cultivate gratitude.* Consider wearing or displaying
  something to symbolize gratitude. This might be a
  piece of jewelry, a note on your e-mail signature, or
  the background on your phone or laptop. When you
  see it, remember.
- *Receive.* As you go about the day, gratefully receive
  your family, friends, and community, with their
  complicated messiness. Gratefully receive another day
  of life, your daily bread, and the chance to work and
  rest. Even during terrible seasons there are gifts.
- *Record.* Keep a gratitude list, and add to it as often as
  possible. You might jot things down in a journal, pin

them to a bulletin board, post them to social media, or simply say them out loud.

Sing to him, sing praise to him;
tell of all his wonderful acts.
Glory in his holy name;
let the hearts of those who seek the LORD rejoice.
Look to the LORD and his strength;
seek his face always.

I CHRONICLES 16:9-11

Music

Music is a powerful tool. Depending on how we use it, music can lift our spirits up to rejoicing or sink us deep into despair. The music we have on in the background of our computers or thoughts profoundly impacts the way we interact with life. Similar to gratitude, music significantly impacts our moods, perception, creativity, memory, intelligence, health, and even pain levels! And thanks to technology, all the music we can imagine is just a click of a button away.

My husband and I received bad news several years ago. It wasn't a life-or-death situation, but it had a huge impact on our family stability. We were in a state of shock for a few days, and then it occurred to us to sing. I started singing "You Are the Living Word" by Fred Hammond and "Made Me Glad" by Hillsong Worship. My husband joined in, and we sang these songs over and over again for weeks. Bit by bit, we remembered hope, we remembered the hands that hold us. We had trials to walk through that took years to overcome, and we had a great deal of work to do. But we kept these two songs with us, and they helped us persevere.

PRACTICE

- *Sing.* Even if you aren't musically talented, lift up your voice! Sing when you're alone, sing with your kids, sing in the park, sing in church, sing in the car, sing while you wash dishes and while you mow the lawn. Just as exercise gets our bodies moving, singing gets our spirits moving—and makes us stronger.

- *Listen.* We might not have time to sit quietly and meditate on truth, but we can have it playing in the background almost any time and everywhere we go. Put together playlists that lift your spirit to God, and keep them on hand. Worship music is a great place to start, but don't be afraid to think outside the box too. What rhythms and melodies lead your body and soul to praise?

- *Choose wisely.* Considering the strong impact music has on us, keep an eye on your musical diet. Destructive messages lurk behind enticing rhythms, and while the emotional catharsis of angry, bitter, or depressing songs can be tempting, make sure to include plenty of hope, joy, and love.

I will sing to the LORD all my life;
  I will sing praise to my God as long as I live.

PSALM 104:33

CHAPTER 9

CELEBRATION

Alive and Awake

MY FAMILY SETTLES into our seats just as the Christmas service begins. My four-year-old daughter, lovely in the shimmering velvet dress she put on herself, climbs up to stand on the chair. A choir is singing on stage, and she wants to see them. Realizing she knows the song, she begins to sing along to "O Holy Night."

There she stands, a small but determined person towering alone in the crowd, singing. She is gorgeous, precious. The light shines through her hair and reflects off her bright eyes. Her innocent, joy-filled face is given over entirely to the expanding music as it builds. She is pure rejoicing without self-consciousness.

It is a priceless moment, one of the best in my entire life. Tears fill my eyes and spill over as I sit there, watching her sweet face beaming as she sings with all her might. Some piece of my soul will be sitting in this sweet moment for eternity.

But five minutes later the song ends. She climbs down from her perch and sprawls on daddy's lap, complaining about this or that. Five more minutes and we're "one more chance" shy of leaving the service.

Isn't this motherhood exactly? Isn't this life precisely? The beauty and the pain, always arriving in one bittersweet package. The darkness can seem endless, but the sorrowful never entirely outshines the beautiful. There is a Light that cannot be snuffed out. There is a Love that always wins.

And it does peek through occasionally.

My beautiful, precocious daughter wore me out that morning with the naughty chaos that ensued, and I left the church that day with relief. So many occasions that begin beautifully wear me out; so often I'm relieved when the hours of another precious day come to an end.

But I will never, ever forget the way her eyes shone as she stood singing.

Practicing the Presence of God

You know the feeling: You've just entered the warm house on a cold day, into the beckoning scent of your favorite dinner. Or after hiking for hours through mountains, you turn and discover the summit, gasping at the unexpected view.

Think of slowly savoring the first bite of your favorite thing to eat—of breathing in the scent of an exotic wine, then taking an indulgent sip. Imagine hugging someone you've been longing to see or experiencing a moment so special you stop everything else and just take it all in.

These are single moments, lasting only a breath. Yet they are remarkable and impact our memory because of their power. We make them even more memorable by savoring them, by moving for a second in slow motion. Past and future flee from our minds, and we fully embrace this one moment. We embrace *being alive right here right now.* Just as we are always breathing but rarely aware of it, similarly we are always existing but rarely conscious of it.

But in these brief and wonderful seconds, we are startled entirely into consciousness.

When I was in labor with my daughter, my sons were vomiting. By the time I delivered, they had what we assumed was a severe cold as well. Bringing home our newborn felt like a reckless act, and we kept her separate as much as possible. Still, we all—children, parents, grandparents—came down with the nasty virus. Everyone but the tiny newborn.

After two weeks we figured the boys were healthy enough to see and touch and hold their baby sister, and since I was sick myself, there seemed no point in continuing the quarantine. So we commenced with the hugging and snuggling, small hands bravely holding a tiny sister for the first time.

Then the pediatrician called. We had all tested positive for pertussis.

I still see spots when I remember this conversation. We were all vaccinated; I hadn't seen it coming at all.

By the time the call came, we were on the mend but still contagious and exposing our baby girl. Already worn thin with a newborn, postpartum issues, sick kids, and illness, we entered a blur of doctor's appointments, trips to the pharmacy, and interviews with the County Health Department. But mostly there was me cradling my infant, staring at the ceiling, petrified with disbelief and anxiety. All the conversations with doctors and health departments reinforced what I already knew, what often happens when newborns and pertussis mix.

In the midst of all this we had water leaking into the basement, into the attic, even a pond in our family room one night.

I survived the same way I endured labor and delivery: When the contraction (or crisis) peaks, throw yourself into it and get through it. When it abates, even though it's not over, even though a bigger and harder one is coming at any moment, refuse to panic. Relax while you can.

Whenever someone was not actually throwing up or water was not actively leaking and no one was close enough to cough on the baby, I pictured bright lights to keep the darkness—always so close to a postpartum mother—at bay.

Then I woke in the night, vomiting myself. Between heaves I said to my husband, "We have a lot of challenges right now."

But vomiting forced me to stay in the disgustingly tactile moment so entirely that my anxiety went down, just a bit. I still watched and worked just as hard to keep my daughter safe, but focusing on keeping food down kept the debilitating worry at bay.

Grace, in the form of vomit.

This unusual gift allowed my heavy eyes to find other silver linings in those deeply cloudy days: the huge, beaming smile on my son's face as he held and talked to his baby sister for the first time (there has never been a smile so big, so beautiful). My other son asking to hold her, always the first to sing to her if he saw a frown. And—in the truest test of his heart—inviting her along when he went off to do big-kid stuff.

The more silver linings I saw, the more I became conscious of them. Holding my daughter when she smiled at me for the first time and tried to chatter. The precious way newborns stretch when you hold them up in the air—hands in fists and arms raised high, feet and legs lifted up pretzel style in midair. The sleepy, satisfied look on her face in the seconds after nursing. How entirely precious, loved, and beautiful my vulnerable, embodied children are.

One of the underlying convictions of the spiritual life is that God is in our midst, and we carry out our lives in his loving, sustaining presence. Our challenge is to *awaken* to this reality, to remember it, to keep company with him even in our busyness and darkness. To *practice* the daily presence of God.

We don't practice disciplines to compel him, to please him with our efforts or convince him to come be with us. He is here, he made us, he longs for relationship with us. The disciplines are to compel *ourselves*; to train our anxious, busy minds to quiet in his presence; to rest like a well-fed infant in his arms.

We are not alive for long, any of us. I, for one, don't want to miss it.

We can live a distracted life, or we can go about our days realizing the presence of the One who offers abundant life. He can, from the rubble of our tasks, anxiety, and noise, build a sanctuary—an open space of peace and love and worship in the midst of our diaper bags, grocery bags, and laptop bags. He can show us the silver traces in our darkness.

My daughter, not a month old at the time and entirely oblivious to so much work and worry on her behalf, never got sick. I am forever grateful for this unmerited gift.

Rejoice Therapy

The apostle Paul lived before Twitter became a thing, but if he'd had access to social media I can imagine him tweeting, "Rejoice in the Lord always. I will say it again: Rejoice!" (Philippians 4:4).

I doubt his message would have gone viral; it's a bit too

perky. But this is not a case of over-optimism. The man who wrote these words was in prison; the people he addressed were confronting life-altering difficulties of all kinds. And Paul was not alone—every book of the New Testament carries this theme: *Rejoice in the Lord.* Not because we are naively privileged and have no real sense of sorrow or suffering. No, we are called to rejoice because God's joyous presence *is*. And through the practice of celebrating, we learn to see it and embrace it and fan it into flame.

Have you ever undergone physical therapy? I once had to relearn the use of my left hand, and the therapy required was *painful*. It wasn't fun; it was *suffering*. I didn't go to the therapist because I took so much joy in bending my broken fingers again and again, but because I had so much pain in the practice.

Likewise, we don't draw our attention to the daily miracles of life and beauty because we are so peaceful and joyful, but because we are miserable, tense, and worried. Celebration is *practice*, and spiritual disciplines are physical therapy for the soul. With each painful repetition we gain a bit more mobility, a bit more strength. We wouldn't need so many reminders to rejoice unless we so often *didn't* feel like rejoicing. Mindful celebration is how we turn our troubled spirits to God and choose life. One tiny baby step at a time.

Like when I'm rushing to the store and make a left-hand turn onto the highway, right into the most magnificent sunset. Or when I'm walking down the sidewalk and notice the beads of dew still clinging to the velvet-soft leaves of my newly budding trees. Or when I'm interrupted after bedtime *again* the evening before my deadline and notice how sweet my girl looks in her footie pajamas.

Of course, this might not be enough. There may be deep problems that plague your spirit, that call for radical interventions. After all, cancer is not cured by physical therapy! If you are experiencing abuse, you need help and a major life change. If you're experiencing depression or a mental illness, you need competent, compassionate clinical help. But throughout it all, celebration is the daily practice that will make us stronger, that will shine a bit more light into our spirits, day after difficult day.

Yes, we rejoice in these everyday miracles not because we are so happy, but because we desperately need the practice.

The Snakes

I enter Myrtle's room quietly. She is old, bound to a wheelchair, and spends most of her days alone. Her mind is busy—but elsewhere. She cannot see the room around her, only the rooms that haunt her hallucinating memory in a mind long gone.

She calls to me, urgently. "The snakes!" she shrieks. "The floor is covered in snakes!" I am by her side, taking her hand in my hands, directing her eyes to my face, speaking words of assurance—but she cannot find me with any of her failing senses. Instead, she trembles with fear, crying out to someone she believes is far away, "Please help me! The snakes are everywhere!"

Then, believing that no help is coming, she begins to sing:

Why should I be discouraged, why should the shadows come?
Why should my heart be lonely, and long for heaven and
*   home,*
When Jesus is my portion? My constant friend is He:
His eye is on the sparrow, and I know He watches me.[13]

Her caregiver, she believes, has not come to help. The snakes, she knows, are everywhere, filling the room and surrounding her chair; she can't escape them on her own. But deep inside her soul is a place unmarred by her body and mind's betrayal. She is not a victim of these dire circumstances. She cannot be, for her soul is embedded in the presence of God.

And so, in terror and desperation, she does the same thing she does every day in this situation. She sings to Jesus.

It doesn't matter, really, that her room is clean and safe, that I am there to help, that this scenario has played out a hundred times. The reality in her mind is the truth. Left alone in a terrifying scenario, she determinedly sings her way to peace. As she repeats the promises and assurances in each verse, her body eases. The song does its work, and after a while Myrtle can see me, hear me, feel me. The snakes have left.

She is safe again, and it is nearly time for lunch.

———·—

I don't know Myrtle's history, what trials and nightmares she passed through to learn such deep strength and reliance on God's presence. But years of practice have produced a lovely and fragrant harvest that weighs down the branches of her remaining years. Myrtle can turn fear for her life into a song of trust in God because she spent a lifetime practicing. This is not the sort of skill you get right on the first try.

Just as my children rehearse scales and ball dribbling, there is value in *practicing* spiritual disciplines. A life spent cultivating prayer and service, meditation and worship, fasting and celebration, will reap a harvest. Our mommy days are fertile ground for this practicing, because our mundane moments are ripe with opportunities to lose our grip, our patience, ourselves.

Recovering the Missing Stories

Have you heard of the Proverbs 31 woman? She's the renowned subject of a poem that concludes the book of Proverbs. This poem extols her hard work and wisdom, calling her a woman of excellence and worth. Unfortunately, the legendary "Proverbs 31 woman" is most often used as a very specific but nearly impossible standard for modern-day women to please God (and their husbands).

Author Rachel Held Evans has written extensively on the gap between the intended and popular use of this poem. In her research she discovered the intent behind this biblical passage:

calling husbands to sing the praises of their wives' everyday efforts. Rather than a prescriptive-but-unreachable standard, Proverbs 31, "like any good poem, . . . is [meant] to draw attention to the often-overlooked glory of the everyday."[14]

We mothers are often far too tired and stretched far too thin. We put hopes for spiritual advancement on the back burner for the time being, fully aware that the traditional disciplines of meditation, prayer, fasting, study, and so many more have fallen out of our grasp.

But as with the poem in Proverbs 31, the purpose of spiritual exercise has always been to infuse daily life with opportunities to practice placing our eyes on God rather than on ourselves—loosening our grip on everything else and falling into him.

Motherhood does this on its own, each and every day, if we let it. So, what if we take our focus off what we fail to do and instead awaken to the efforts we put forth every single day?

Motherhood may keep us from the traditional disciplines but only by offering a banquet table spread with spiritually formative adventures. Through the seasons of creation, incarnation, and nurture; through the days of waiting, loss, surrender, sacrifice, rejoicing, service, solitude, isolation, suffering, perseverance, and celebration, the tools we need are *already here*. We don't need to put aside our creaturely existence to find him on some holy plane. He is waiting for us *here*, inviting us to rest in the nurturing arms of the One who invented the idea of mothers and fathers and children—who came to earth not as a powerful deity but as a baby, formed in Mary's womb, born into her waiting arms, and nourished by her aching breasts.

Whether your daily tasks entail carrying a pregnant belly, rocking an infant, chasing a toddler, or driving a school child; whether you struggle to balance your career with family or your sanity with your children's needs; whether you met your children in the birthing room or the adoption room—your journey is of great spiritual value.

Sister, you have joined the ranks of life-givers that stretch back to the dawn of time. Women who rose early, cradled babies, carried water, boiled rice. Mothers who scrubbed linens and built fires, who dreaded infertility and longed for their lost children, who cuddled toddlers and scolded naughty offspring. These adventures have stretched from generation to generation, and though they have rarely been written into glorious epics, they have formed the backbone of human life and spirit. These women's stories may be missing from our history and theology books, but they are no less real, no less valuable, no less true—and they are not forgotten.

We tell them with our own lives each and every day.

Alive and Awake

My children are at the park on a warm, sunny day, the first after months of cold, housebound weeks. Each of us feels like a newborn lamb trying out new legs, struck with joy at the beauty of the day, the fresh breath of air, the ability to move our strong bodies. As I stand watching, the three of them hike to the top of a grassy hill, pause—and run.

Down, down, down they go, legs pumping, arms flailing, hair flying. Down, down, down. Faces turned toward the blue sky, they worship God as creation always has done: by fully accepting his gift of life and *being*. By existing boldly and joyfully just as he made them.

Some days, just walking outside and breathing the fresh air is a prayer, a song of worship.

Friend, each day of our lives has this. The brilliant sun may be buried behind miles of clouds, cold, and storm, but it is shining, sustaining our life. The joys of creation may be concealed by layers of depression and trouble—but joy is here nonetheless. *He* is here.

Months may pass between sightings. Then the clouds will part and the sun's rays will shine down, if only for a moment before hiding again. You'll notice the heart your daughter drew in preschool, just for you, or the sun shining off your toddler's hair. We almost miss, but then notice, how tall and strong our growing children look today or how tenderly they lean over to kiss us before school.

However hidden and fleeting, these moments are here, and they point us to the bedrock of reality: Our Creator made this good creation and came to rest among us. He joined us physically in womb, birth, daily muddy life, and death. He went further than we have yet gone, leading the way to redemption and resurrection. Our King has never condemned or belittled us mortals, asking us to ascend to his level; he came to ours. And he has *never* condemned or belittled women, considering us second rate, undeserving, or dirty. He announced both his conception and his resurrection—his life and his new life—first of all to women. And he called us into a sacred partnership in his own beloved tasks of creation and nurture.

We are not unseen. He himself is the one who sees us.

On this day so full of joy and difficulty, work and rest, I celebrate *you*, sister, honored mother. You, with all your flaws and impatience, courage and feisty determination, nurture and nagging insecurities. You are a woman of God, a daughter, a creator.

May you always stand tall and sing.

CELEBRATION IN PRACTICE

See

How often do we look at something without seeing? Budding trees in the yard and people in the store aisles, a pattern of cracking paint on the wall and the expression on a child's face—we tend to just speed on by without fully noticing what's before us day by day.

We use our eyes constantly, and we move so fast. Making quick surface judgments, we miss the depth and complexity of knowing and the wisdom found in the process of knowing. When we let ourselves encounter the reality around us—watching kids playing; observing the road while driving; or looking deeply at the walls, floors, and furniture around us—we can learn to take in and receive the life before us. There is a spiritual discipline of *seeing* we can practice each and every day.

PRACTICE

- *Look.* We can't see if we don't look. When you have the chance, spend a moment taking it all in. Is there a tree outside your window? Look at it while you brush your teeth, and observe what happens. Is your son bombarding you with questions while you cook dinner? While the pot simmers, take a second to turn and *look* at him.
- *Make eye contact.* As you pass other humans making their way through the grocery aisle, parking lot, or sidewalk, acknowledge them with eye contact, a smile, or a door held open. Remember that this person, though a stranger, is created in the image of God and is deeply loved. This stranger is part of our community of creation.
- *Receive.* Take in the beauty and wisdom all around you, and use concrete, material nature to ground you in the present. As you walk from the car to the

building, consider the sky and the soil. Realize the ground you step on. Notice the child trotting behind you. Receive the calming blessing of being and the mundane silver linings in every day.

If you call out for insight
  and cry aloud for understanding,
and if you look for it as for silver
  and search for it as for hidden treasure,
then you will . . . find the knowledge of God.

PROVERBS 2:3-5

Hear

We are bombarded by sounds every moment. We simply cannot shut our ears. Our lives offer very few moments that are entirely silent; even if we escape all people, animals, birds, and bugs, our own heart will be pounding, our stomach growling, our lungs filling with air.

Bombarded as we are by sound, we filter out most of what we hear by necessity. Taking in even a fraction of the noise around us would lead to insanity. Yet learning to *listen* and *hear* is a rich meditative practice. Though we might prefer an hour or two of silence, moms are far more likely to find chaos. What if we took the raw materials we have and practiced deeply hearing the sounds around us?

The white noises of appliances and heating vents can be soothing. Trains and traffic sounds can be strangely comforting. Children and family echoes mean life and belonging. And we can almost always hear the chirping of birds, barking of dogs, and humming of bugs to remind us of the created world we're part of.

Here, too, is a rich feast for our spirits—if we can awaken to it.

PRACTICE

- *Listen to the noise.* Have you ever sat and tried to identify all the noises in the background? Listening can be deeply meditative if we do it mindfully. Close your eyes for a moment and name the individual sounds around you. The wind blowing through the leaves, the dryer humming downstairs, the radio across the street. We hear but don't hear these on a regular basis; sorting through them one by one is an accessible but powerful way to stay present in the moment.
- *Listen to others.* It is so easy to avoid focusing on what the person before us is really saying, with words, tone, body, and face. Practice being present with whoever is before you, hearing deeply. Of course, this is challenging when your son has just scraped his leg and your daughter is begging to go potty. Be patient with yourself—this is practice, not perfection.
- *Listen to yourself.* Part of the practice of hearing is learning to hear ourselves. What is your mood or anxiety trying to tell you? Why so eager or hesitant? Though we may need to coach rather than indulge ourselves, we

won't be effective at either one if we haven't first learned to hear what our body and spirit are trying to say.

Incline your ear, and come to me;
hear, that your soul may live.
ISAIAH 55:3, ESV

Touch

Personal space and mothers go together like peanut butter and horseshoes—in other words, hardly ever. We moms are touching soft skin, being tugged on by anxious hands and jumped on by rambunctious bundles of energy. These thousands of touch points can go unnoticed or build up to annoyance. Either way, here too we can be mindful of what we touch and how, as well as what is touching us. We are impacting and being impacted each and every time.

In a way, the first and last practices of this book encompass the spirit of all the others in between. Whatever else we may be doing, we are breathing, walking, seeing, hearing, touching, *being*. Moms may not have time for elaborately creative strategies of devotional practice, but even in this life season we participate fully in these building blocks of existence. These are the things we are doing, so let's follow Scripture's advice and do them unto the Lord. While the commotion of demands on our time and attention may keep us from stepping consciously into them, we can awaken, bit by bit, day by day, and use these daily things to cultivate the fruit of the Spirit.

We are alive, and we are not alone. By touching we receive, give, and connect. *Touch* the children surrounding you. *Touch* the dishes and laundry piled up. *Touch* the fork as you lift it. *Touch* the friend or family member sharing life with you. Find in your fingers the confirmation of life and living in the presence of God.

PRACTICE

- *Touch mindfully.* Whatever tasks surround you today, try to remember to feel the things you are touching, whether the phone beneath your finger, the ground beneath your feet, or the child inside your embrace.
- *Caress lovingly.* At least once today, use your touch to express love, peace, and grace. Whether you are touching another person, holding an object in your house, or putting on your own socks, allow your touch to be life-giving.
- *Practice with patience.* Remember that in all these things, we are practicing. There is no benefit here if we feel loaded down by more "should haves" and burden. Instead, focus on the time or two that you remember to *touch*, and be grateful.

Oh, taste and see that the LORD is good!
PSALM 34:8, ESV

One Last Thing . . .

Before you go, can we talk about one last thing?

Sister, let's be honest. Most of history, spirituality, theology, and the stories of society were not written by mothers. No, generally speaking, life has been interpreted and recorded by people who rarely observed and never experienced the way life and death ebbs and flows in our bodies each month—people who have not experienced the creation and nurture, sacrifice and surrender, service and perseverance that overcome a mother's body and soul.

God formed our bodies *on purpose* and called them *good*. In the seasons of life he gives us, we encounter and know a unique part of God and his creation that *cannot be known* without our voice, without our teaching. We represent a part of God's image that the world cannot see except by looking at his work in and through us. Our voice is necessary, our wisdom is indispensable, and both of these are beautiful and lovely and true.

And so, it is not for ourselves only that we pay attention

to these things our Creator has given us and asked of us. Our daughters and sisters need to know, and our brothers need to know also. Our sons need to know, along with our fathers. The world needs to learn from these truths that teach and form us. What we are living is not merely "female truth"—it is *truth*.

Sisters, we are the only ones equipped to tell this story, to testify to this truth, to tell of this wisdom—to the entire world.

Our Creator invited us to meet him here, in our bodies. He designed the biological processes of attraction and sex, pregnancy and birth; he created our fierce protective love—in fact, he placed his own fierce love inside us. All these organic, day-to-day pieces that turn our bodies and souls into mothers come from him, and he has always been here with us.

Find him here. Find him here and throw yourself into his beautiful arms. He is always, always waiting to catch you.

Then live your story, sister. Live it bravely and fully.

Acknowledgments

WRITING THIS BOOK has been its own spiritual discipline, and as with any practice, I needed a strong community to keep me going. Thank you to everyone who came alongside me—this book is yours, too.

Matthew, when I found you reading that first draft, moved to tears by my words, everything changed. Your overflowing enthusiasm gave me the strength to believe this book could come to life. Thank you for your exuberant faith in me. Your love and partnership is built into every piece; I could not have done any of this without you. You are in all these pages.

Aubrey Sampson, you are the gracious and tireless midwife of this book. Remember all those chats (and hand wringing) over coffee and the heads of our loud, wiggly children? Thank you for your friendship from that day until now. You are a true gift from God, and I'm so grateful to be on the writing journey with you.

My beautiful, powerful Redbud sisters: In so many ways this book would not exist without you. Terri, Aleah, and

Afton, thank you for getting out and pushing me uphill when I refused to start the engine. And all the rest of you, too many to name: We go further together.

Mandy, Farrah, Heather, Katharine, and Kristen—you are my sister-mamas, my kindred spirits. Thank you for the countless ways you speak into my life, encouraging me and loving me as is. I wish every mother could have the life-giving community that I have with you.

My agent, Don Gates. Thank you for hearing me out and catching the vision. Your excitement made me excited. Thank you for all your work on my behalf.

My brilliant editor, Caitlyn Carlson, and all the wonderful folks at NavPress and Tyndale. From your first e-mail and phone call, I knew my book had found a home with you. You made this process a joy from start to finish, and I'm so grateful to have landed here with you.

Thank you to the countless women and mothers who have poured themselves into me as I learned how to be a mama; who cleaned my house, watched my children, and brought me meals. Thank you for asking the right questions ("Are you sleeping? Are you eating?") instead of the painful ones ("Are you loving every minute?"). Most of all, thank you to my own mothers, for life and a million unseen gifts: Linda and Beverly, Irma, Hattie, and Ruth. I stand on the shoulders of such a great cloud of witnesses. And Dad, thank you for pondering the Bible and theology out loud while a little girl sat on your lap. I was listening.

And last but never least, thank you, our Creator and

Sustainer, the One who was, and is, and is to come. Thank you for revealing yourself to us as mother and father. I pray that I have spoken of you faithfully and well.

For I also remember the voice that came to John in Patmos, saying, what thou seest, write it in a book, and though I do not dare to claim a knowledge of this voice, yet do I dare to claim a knowledge of some voice. Therefore I put aside my fears, and am obedient.

ALAN PATON, *Too Late the Phalarope*

Notes

1. Richard Foster, *Celebration of Discipline* (New York: HarperCollins, 1998).
2. St. Benedict, edited by Timothy Fry, *The Rule of St. Benedict in English* (Collegeville, MN: Liturgical Press, 1982), 69.
3. Sara Given, *It's Like They Know Us* (blog), http://itsliketheyknowus.tumblr.com/ (accessed August 2016).
4. John J. Parsons, "God as 'El Shaddai,'" Hebrew for Christians, http://www.hebrew4christians.com/Scripture/Parashah/Summaries/Lekh_Lekha/El_Shaddai/el_shaddai.html (accessed August 9, 2016).
5. God also describes himself in this passage with "Yet he does not leave the guilty unpunished; he punishes the children and their children for the sin of the parents to the third and fourth generation." This is heavy language, and addressing it fully is outside the scope of the chapter, but I will say this: Apart from spanning multiple generations, it also describes the work of a parent!
6. "Prayer in the Evening: Attributed to St. Augustine," in *Prayer Book for Catholics*, ed. Jacquelyn Lindsey (Huntington, IN: Our Sunday Visitor, 2005), 92.
7. Foster, *Celebration of Discipline*, 130.
8. Thomas Hale, *Applied New Testament Commentary* (Colorado Springs: David C Cook, 2007), 397.
9. Reinhold Niebuhr, *The Essential Reinhold Niebuhr* (New Haven, CT: Yale University Press, 1986), 251.
10. Eugene Peterson, *A Long Obedience in the Same Direction* (Downers Grove, IL: InterVarsity Press, 1980, 2000).
11. Peterson, *A Long Obedience in the Same Direction*, 131.
12. Paraphrased from Chumbawamba, "Tubthumping," *Tubthumper* © 1997 by Sony/ATV Music Publishing.
13. Civilla D. Martin, "His Eye Is on the Sparrow," 1905, public domain.
14. Rachel Held Evans, "3 Things You Might Not Know about Proverbs 31," RachelHeldEvans.com, May 12, 2014, http://rachelheldevans.com/blog/3-things-you-might-not-know-about-proverbs-31 (accessed February 6, 2016).

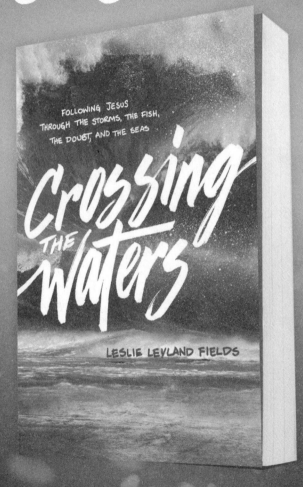